CW01261567

POSITIVE ENERGY POSITIVE LIFE

The Power of Optimism & Self-Love

SIDDHARTH BANDYOPADHYAY

Copyright © 2023 Siddharth Bandyopadhyay

All rights reserved

No part of this book may be reproduced, or stored in a retrieval system, or transmitted in any form or by any means, electronic, mechanical, photocopying, recording, or otherwise, without the express written permission of the author.

ISBN: 9798850370053

DEDICATION

In the depths of my heart, I dedicate this book to my extraordinary parents, whose steadfast presence and boundless love have shaped me into the person I am today. To my remarkable mother, whose nurturing spirit and belief in my abilities have instilled in me a profound sense of self-love and the courage to follow the path less travelled. To my extraordinary father, whose relentless pursuit of growth and determination to embrace new horizons have inspired me to push beyond my limits and unlock my true potential. Without their unwavering support and unfaltering faith, this literary journey would have remained a distant dream. I am forever indebted to them for their enduring love, unwavering guidance, and the invaluable lessons they have bestowed upon me.

PURPOSE

This book is your transformative guide, illuminating the path towards a life brimming with positivity, joy, and self-empowerment. It invites you to embark on a profound journey of self-discovery, where the remarkable power of optimism and the nurturing embrace of self-love will unlock your limitless potential. Through inspiring stories, practical exercises, and empowering guidance, this book equips you with the tools to radiate positive energy, reframe challenges, and cultivate deep inner peace. Get ready to embrace a life that overflows with positivity, abundance, and authentic self-love. Let the pages of "Positive Energy Positive Life" be your radiant companion on this transformative journey towards a life of positivity and fulfilment.

CONTENTS

CHAPTER 1

The Basics of Positive Energy 1

The Benefits of Cultivating Positive Energy 7

How to Identify Negative Energy in your Life..........13

Removing Negative Energy......................... 17

Boosting Positive Energy: Transforming Mindsets and Practices...22

CHAPTER 2

The Power of Optimism 31

Essence of Optimism 34

Dispelling Misconceptions about Optimism............36

The Benefits of Optimism 38

How to Cultivate Optimism in Your Daily Life 45

Sustaining Optimism: Practical Strategies in Tough Times 48

Triumph through Optimism: Personal Stories of Overcoming Adversity 52

CHAPTER 3

The Importance of Self-Love 63

The Benefits of Self-Love 65

How to Cultivate Self-Love In Your Daily Life ... 69

Embracing Imperfections: Emphasising Self-Acceptance and Growth 73

Self-Love Transformations: Personal Stories of Change 76

CHAPTER 4

The Role of Mindfulness 81

The Benefits of Mindfulness 85

Techniques for Practicing Mindfulness 91

Mindfulness Journeys: Stories Of Peace And Clarity..96

CHAPTER 5

Gratitude and Positive Self-Talk 101

The Science of Gratitude: Exploring Psychological & Physical Benefits 106

Techniques For Practising Gratitude 109

Techniques for Practicing Positive Self-Talk 112

Life Transformations: Gratitude and Self-Talk Stories 116

CHAPTER 6

The Power of Forgiveness 121

The Benefits of Forgiveness 124

The Role of Self-Forgiveness 128

Techniques for Practicing Forgiveness 131

Healing Through Forgiveness: Personal Stories of Freedom 142

CHAPTER7

Overcoming Fear & Anxiety 145

Identifying Fear and Anxiety 149

Techniques for Overcoming Fear & Anxiety 153

Building Resilience: Strategies for Nurturing Mental Strength 159

Conquering Fear: Inspiring Stories of Dream Achievement 163

CHAPTER8

The Importance of Connection 173

Dangers of Isolation 176

Benefits of Cultivating Connection 181

Building Meaningful Relationships 185

Community Power: Inspiring Personal Stories 190

CHAPTER 9

Living with Purpose 197

Techniques for Discovering Your Purpose 204

The Impact of Living with Purpose on Mental & Emotional Well-being 207

The Role of Gratitude in Living a Purposeful Life 210

Pursuit of Purpose: Personal Stories of Fulfilment & Joy 213

CHAPTER 10

Maintaining a Positive Life....................219

Nurturing Positive Relationships: The Power of Connection 224

Self-Care & Well-Being Practices: Sustaining Positive Energy 232

Finding Meaning and Purpose in Everyday Life 239

Eternal Positivity: Inspiring Personal Stories 244

CHAPTER 11

Cultivating Positivity with Everyday Things 253

Using Arts, Colours, Space Design & Clothing 255

Spreading Positive Energy: The Power of Simple Actions 260

Harnessing the Power of Music for Positive Vibes 261

CONCLUSION 265

REFERENCES 271

INTRODUCTION

Positivity is a precious gift and culture that is often underrated, whereas it is the difference between a person's quality of life. Surely, we see people who have high education, socioeconomic status, and many nice things, but are bitter, live in suspicion, and are not having the best of life. On the other hand, we have seen people who have fewer feats that are living happily and affecting their world. That's the power of positivity, and that is why we need to understand it. There are times we feel like we are stuck, some other times we are just going through the motions but not really living. In those moments, we may open ourselves to negativity unknown to us. Many other times, those feelings and experiences are pointers to us we have been living in negativity. Positive energy is like a gentle breeze that has the power to lift us from the darkest depths and carry us towards a brighter tomorrow. It radiates from within us, impacting every aspect of our lives. Embracing positivity invites a cascade of transformation into our relationships, our careers, and our overall well-being.

> "The science of positive energy is both simple and profound: when we uplift others, we ourselves are uplifted."
>
> — Dacher Keltner

The concept of positivity came out of the concept of vibes and energy. The philosophy of vibes and energy is a belief that everything in the universe is made up of energy, and that our thoughts, feelings, and actions can affect the energy around us (Rupp, 2013[1]). This energy can be positive or negative, and it can have a direct impact on our physical and emotional well-being. This concept has philosophical, scientific, religious, and traditional backing as we are going to explore in this book. Regardless of where you pitch your tent, whether scientific, religious or otherwise, you will discover that vibes and energy are a more fundamental part of reality, and that they can be used to explain everything from the laws of physics to the workings of the human mind. Irrespective of how you choose to think about them, vibes and energy are a powerful force that can have a big impact on our lives. When we are surrounded by positive vibes, we tend to feel happier, healthier, and more successful. On the other hand, when we are surrounded by negative vibes, we tend to feel stressed, anxious, and depressed. The good news is that we have the power to control the vibes and energy in our lives.

For me, writing this book is more than putting words together to encourage people. I have enjoyed the profound benefits of living a positive life. This book is also a step further in my quest to empower myself with positive energy. At some points in my life, l lived with negative energy. I was trapped in a cycle of pessimism, constantly berating myself and drowning in a sea of low self-esteem. It appeared happiness was an elusive dream, slipping through my fingers no matter how desperately I grasped for it. I was always complaining about my life, my job, my relationships, the government, the neighbourhood, and everything else in between. I was constantly comparing myself to others and feeling like I wasn't good enough. I was also very critical of myself, and would beat myself up over every minor mistake I made. This negative mindset had a profound impact on my life. With a constant feeling of stress and anxiety, I had a hard time enjoying anything. It was hard for me to really connect with other people back then, and I felt like I was always on the outside looking in. However, they are all in the past now. Living positively has changed who I am and how I live. It started when I saw a Facebook video of man giving testimony of how he came out of depression and negativity by harnessing the power of positive energy. Then I decided I was going to change my life too, because I was exhausted from being negative. As I began to read motivational books and articles, watch videos, and listen to podcasts on positive thinking, I began to practise what I learned, and here we are today.

It wasn't easy at first, but slowly but steadily, I started to see a difference. I was less stressed and anxious, and I started to enjoy life more. I also started connecting with other people more easily, and I felt like I finally belonged. I'm still not perfect, and I still have a few negative moments occasionally. Nevertheless, I'm so much happier and more fulfilled now than I ever was when I was a negative person. I know you can change your life too. It won't be easy, but it is possible. All you have to do is start by making a decision to be positive. The effects of positive energy ripple through our interactions with others. It creates a magnetism that draws people towards us, forming deeper connections and fostering a sense of belonging. By radiating positivity, we inspire and uplift those around us, creating a domino effect of joy and fulfilment. Relationships flourish, conflicts dissolve, and a sense of harmony fills the spaces we inhabit, including our career and academics.

Furthermore, the impact of positive energy extends far beyond external circumstances. It permeates our inner world, nourishing our mental, emotional, and physical well-being. By cultivating a positive mindset, we silence the critical voice within and replace it with self-compassion and acceptance. We learn to appreciate our strengths, acknowledge our achievements, and embrace our imperfections as a beautiful part of our unique journey. Now, as I reflect on my own transformation, I am reminded of the words of Maya Angelou, who once said, *"If you don't like something, change it. If you can't change it, change your attitude."* This simple yet profound truth encapsulates the essence of positive energy. It empowers us to take control of our lives, to rewrite our stories, and to rewrite the narratives that hold us back.

In this book, we will delve into the power of positive energy and how it can change your life. We will explore the science, philosophy, and cultures behind it, draw inspiration from renowned authors and thought leaders, and share personal experiences that highlight the transformative nature of embracing positivity so that you can build a sustainable system of positivity around you. My hope is that through these pages, you will find solace, inspiration, and practical tools to harness the power of positive energy and embark on your own remarkable journey of transformation. Together, we will unlock the power of positive energy and create a life filled with joy, purpose, and boundless possibilities.

1
THE BASICS OF POSITIVE ENERGY

"Choosing positive energy opens up possibilities, allowing you to grow and flourish in ways you never imagined."

– Barbara Fredrickson

Positivity is not the same as "*don't worry, be happy*" (Fredrickson, 2009). The concept of positive energy extends beyond psychological and spiritual realms; it also finds resonance in the field of physics. According to physics, energy is a fundamental concept that underlies the functioning of the universe (Chaisson, 2014). Understanding positive energy in this context involves exploring the concept of vibrations and its connection to the universe. In physics, everything in the universe is believed to be in a constant state of vibration. Subatomic particles, atoms, and even larger objects possess a characteristic frequency or vibration. This concept aligns with the idea that positive energy is associated with higher vibrational frequencies, while negative energy corresponds to lower frequencies. The word "vibes" is often used colloquially to refer to the subtle energy or aura that we perceive from people, places, or things. Science has shown that everything in the universe, including humans, is made up of energy.

Positive energy is an intangible force that radiates from within us, influencing our thoughts, emotions, and actions. It is a state of mind characterised by optimism, gratitude, and a genuine belief in the inherent goodness of oneself and others. Positive energy uplifts and inspires, creating a ripple effect that extends to our surroundings. As renowned psychologist Barbara Fredrickson (2009) eloquently puts it, *"Positive energy opens up possibilities, whereas negative energy shuts them down."*

Negative energy, on the other hand, is characterised by pessimism, self-doubt, and a focus on limitations and shortcomings. It weighs us down, drains our vitality, and hampers our ability to flourish. The renowned psychiatrist and Holocaust survivor Viktor Frankl (1946) once said, *"Between stimulus and response, there is a space. In that space lies our freedom and power to choose our response. In our response lies our growth and happiness."* This space he refers to is where we can choose to respond with positive energy, even in the face of adversity.

The relationship between positive energy and vibrations can be seen in the phenomenon of resonance. Resonance occurs when two objects vibrate at the same or harmonically related frequencies, causing an amplification of energy. Similarly, when we align ourselves with positive energy, our vibrations harmonise with the frequencies of the universe, leading to a state of resonance and increased energy flow. Scientific literature provides insights into the connection between positive energy and physical well-being. Jain et al. (2015) explored the effects of positive emotions on heart health, and found that experiencing positive emotions, such as love, gratitude, and joy, was associated with improved cardiovascular health indicators. Tang et al. (2015) published in Nature Reviews Neuroscience demonstrated that mindfulness practice leads to changes in brain activity and neural connectivity associated with emotional regulation and well-being.

Our bodies, thoughts, and emotions are all forms of energy that interact with the environment and with others. This understanding comes from various scientific disciplines, such as physics, biochemistry, and psychology. When it comes to emotions, research has demonstrated a clear connection between vibes and emotional states. Emotions are not just subjective experiences, but are associated with specific physiological changes in our bodies. For instance, when we feel happy, our body releases neurotransmitters like dopamine and serotonin, which create a sense of well-being. These emotional states are not confined to our minds alone, but can be felt by others through subtle cues like facial expressions, body language, and even energetic vibrations.

The phenomenon of emotional contagion further supports the connection between vibes and emotions. Emotional contagion is the process by which we "catch" or synchronise our emotions with those around us. This can happen unconsciously through the subtle energy exchanges that occur during social interactions. When we encounter someone who is radiating positive vibes, it can uplift our own emotional state, whereas encountering someone with negative vibes may influence us to feel more down or drained.

Research in the field of psychology has also explored the impact of positive and negative energy on our well-being. Positive energy, characterised by feelings of joy, love, and gratitude, has been associated with improved mental and physical health, enhanced resilience, and greater overall life satisfaction. On the other hand, negative energy, characterised by emotions like anger, fear, and resentment, can have detrimental effects on our well-being, leading to stress, anxiety, and even physical ailments.

Traditional Chinese Medicine (TCM) and Indian philosophies provide additional insights into the concept of positive energy. In TCM, the notion of Qi (pronounced "chee") represents the vital energy that flows through our bodies and influences our overall well-being. According to TCM, maintaining a balanced and harmonious flow of Qi is crucial for optimal health (Samuels et al., 2008). Positive energy, in this context, is associated with the free and unobstructed movement of Qi, promoting vitality and wellness. In Indian philosophy, the concept of Prana refers to the life force or vital energy that permeates all living beings (Manasa et al., 2020). It is believed that Prana flows through various energy channels in the body known as "nadis". Positive energy, or positive Prana, is associated with the unimpeded flow of this life force, promoting physical, mental, and spiritual health. In both Traditional Chinese medicine and Indian Medicine, when there is a disruption in this natural flow of energy, the body and the mind will suffer illness, consequently it will create an imbalance in the person's life.

The connection between vibes and emotions highlights the importance of being aware of the energy we radiate and absorb from others. By cultivating positive vibes and emotions within ourselves, we not only enhance our own well-being, but also create a ripple effect on those around us. Our energetic state can influence the atmosphere of a room, the dynamics of a group, and even the quality of our relationships. While the science behind vibes and energy is still being explored, many people have experienced firsthand the profound impact of positive vibes on their lives. Practices such as meditation, mindfulness, gratitude, and self-care can help us cultivate positive energy within ourselves and create a more harmonious, energetic resonance with the world.

THE BENEFITS OF CULTIVATING POSITIVE ENERGY

"Happiness is not something readymade. It comes from your own actions."

— Dalai Lama

In the pursuit of understanding the benefits of cultivating positive energy, we can draw inspiration from prominent positive psychologists like Dr. Barbara Fredrickson, Martin Seligman, and many others. Their research has shed light on the profound impact that positive energy can have on our lives, encompassing increased happiness, better health, and improved relationships. Lyubomirsky et al. (2005) indicates that individuals who actively engage in positive thinking experience greater levels of happiness and life satisfaction. Positive energy fuels resilience, empowering us to navigate life's challenges with grace and determination.

Improved Health and Well-Being

Positive energy not only influences our emotional well-being but also has a profound impact on our physical health. Studies by Pressman et al. (2019) suggest that individuals who maintain a positive outlook have a reduced risk of developing cardiovascular diseases. Additionally, research conducted by Moskowitz et al. (2020) reveals that positive emotions can enhance our immune system, leading to improved overall health and longevity.

Opens Up Your Mind

Dr. Barbara Fredrickson, renowned for her work on positive emotions, often emphasises the importance of experiencing a wide range of positive emotions. In her broaden-and-build theory, she suggests that positive emotions, such as joy, gratitude, serenity, interest, hope, pride, amusement, inspiration, awe, and love, broaden our perspective and build lasting personal resources. These positive emotions not only enhance our subjective well-being but also contribute to our psychological resilience and overall life satisfaction (Fredrickson, 2009).

Flourishing

Martin Seligman, considered one of the founding fathers of positive psychology, introduced the concept of flourishing—a state of optimal well-being. Seligman's research highlights the role of positive energy in promoting flourishing, encompassing not only happiness but also a sense of purpose, engagement, positive relationships, and accomplishment (Seligman, 2011). When we cultivate positive energy, we open ourselves up to the possibilities of personal growth, resilience, and a greater sense of fulfilment.

Happiness and Satisfaction

Daniel Kahneman, a Nobel laureate and expert in the field of behavioural economics, has explored the impact of positive energy on our overall well-being. His research suggests that positive experiences and emotions have a significant effect on our subjective happiness, outweighing negative experiences. Kahneman's findings remind us of the importance of nurturing positive energy in our daily lives to enhance our overall happiness and life satisfaction (Kahneman, Diener, & Schwarz, 1999).

Improved Social Connection

Dacher Keltner, a leading expert on the science of emotions, has studied the connection between positive energy and social relationships. His research highlights those positive emotions, such as joy, gratitude, and love, foster social connection, empathy, and pro-social behaviour. By cultivating positive energy, we not only enhance our own well-being, but also contribute to the creation of supportive and fulfilling relationships (Keltner, 2009).

Growth

Carol Dweck's work on mindset further reinforces the importance of positive energy in personal growth and achievement. Dweck's research suggests that adopting a growth mindset, which focuses on the belief that abilities can be developed through effort and practice, leads to greater resilience, perseverance, and success. By embracing positive energy and cultivating a growth mindset, we open ourselves up to greater possibilities and the motivation to continuously learn and grow (Dweck, 2006).

Reduced Stress

The benefits of cultivating positive energy extend beyond subjective well-being. Research has shown psychosocial benefits, such as reduced stress, increased resilience, and improved coping skills (Pressman, Jenkins & Moskowitz, 2019).

Productivity and Success

Socioeconomic benefits have also been observed, with positive energy linked to greater productivity, job satisfaction, and professional success (Lyubomirsky, King, & Diener, 2005). Positive energy plays a vital role in enhancing our quality of life, nurturing positive relationships, and fostering a sense of meaning and purpose.

FOCUS ON GOOD THINGS

I have personally experienced the benefits of positive energy. When I am feeling positive, I am more productive; I am more creative, and I am more resilient. I also have better relationships with the people around me. I have found that the best way to increase positive energy in my life is to focus on the good things and to surround myself with positive people.

As we begin to delve deeper into this book, we will explore practical techniques and strategies for cultivating positive energy, incorporating the wisdom of these positive psychologists and their ground-breaking research. Together, we will discover how embracing positive energy can lead to a life filled with greater happiness, improved health, and more fulfilling relationships. However, before we go further into those practical aspects, it's essential to understand that cultivating positive energy is not about denying or suppressing negative emotions. It's about acknowledging their presence, learning from them, and consciously choosing to focus on the positive aspects of our lives. As Martin Seligman wisely said, "Happiness is not the absence of negative emotions but the presence of positive ones."

Now, you may wonder, how can we identify and remove negative energy from our lives? It starts with self-reflection and awareness.

HOW TO IDENTIFY NEGATIVE ENERGY IN YOUR LIFE

"The greatest discovery of all time is that a person can change his future by merely changing his attitude."

– William James

To harness the power of positive energy, it is essential to identify and remove negative energy from our lives. Reflecting on our experiences and interactions, we can become aware of the sources of negativity that drain our vitality.

Negativity is a personality trait that refers to a tendency to focus on the negative aspects of life. People who are high in negativity are more likely to experience negative emotions, such as anger, sadness, and anxiety (Martin and Dahlen, 2006). They are also more likely to interpret ambiguous situations in a negative way. People who live with negativity are more likely to experience depression, anxiety, and other mental health problems. They are also more likely to have physical health problems, such as heart disease and stroke. In addition, people who are high in negativity are more likely to have problems in their relationships, at work, and in other areas of their lives. Negative energy can manifest in various forms, such as toxic relationships, self-destructive habits, pessimistic thought patterns, or environments that drain our vitality. Recognising and addressing these sources of negativity is a vital step towards creating space for positivity to flourish. As author and speaker Louise Hay (1984) said, *"You have the power to heal your life, and you need to know that. We think so often that we are helpless, but we are not. We always have the power of our minds."*

Identifying negative energy begins with self-reflection and heightened awareness of our thoughts, emotions, and the people and situations that impact us. Paying attention to how we feel in different contexts can provide valuable insights into the presence of negative energy. Notice if certain people consistently bring you down or if certain environments leave you feeling drained and depleted. Reflect on your own thoughts and beliefs. Are there recurring negative patterns or self-critical thoughts that hinder your well-being? In the process of identification, it is essential to approach it with self-compassion and non-judgment. Be assured that negative energy is a natural part of life, and we all encounter it at various times. However, the goal is to develop an understanding of what influences our energy and take proactive steps to remove or mitigate its impact on our lives.

As we embark on this journey of self-discovery and transformation, let us draw inspiration from the words of Eckhart Tolle, renowned spiritual teacher and author: "The primary cause of unhappiness is never the situation but your thoughts about it." Thus, by recognising the power of our thoughts and the impact they have on our energy, we empower ourselves to take control of our experiences. Once we have identified the sources of negative energy, it is time to take steps to remove or minimise their influence in our lives. This process may involve making tough choices, setting boundaries, and nurturing self-care practices that promote positivity. Here are some practical strategies to consider:

Evaluate Relationships

Assess the quality of your relationships and determine if any are consistently draining or toxic. There may be some friends, colleagues or neighbours that make you envy others, make you look down on yourself. Once you observe a constant feeling of uneasiness in your relationship with someone, it is very much likely negative.

Observe Negative Habits

Examine your habits and behaviours that contribute to negative energy. These can include excessive consumption of negative news or media, engaging in self-destructive habits like excessive alcohol or substance use, or engaging in negative self-talk. Sometimes, these habits may be part of you, they go unnoticed. But, when you do a critical analysis of your habits and their triggers, you will know if they are positive or negative.

Evaluate Your Environment

Evaluate your physical surroundings and assess how they impact your energy. Consider decluttering and organising your living and workspace, incorporating elements that inspire and uplift you. Surround yourself with objects, colours, and scents that evoke positivity and serenity.

The journey of removing negative energy is not a one-time event, but an ongoing process of self-discovery and growth. Embrace the willingness to let go of what no longer serves you and make room for positivity to flourish. Recognise that by identifying and releasing negative energy, you regain control over your own wellbeing. Reflect upon this quote by Louise Hay:

"Release the stress. You were never in control anyway."

– Louise Hay

REMOVING NEGATIVE ENERGY: CREATING SPACE FOR POSITIVITY

As we have seen, it is essential to identify the negative energy that may be present in our lives. Negative energy can manifest in various forms, such as toxic relationships, self-destructive habits, pessimistic thought patterns, or environments that drain our vitality. Recognising and addressing these sources of negativity is a vital step towards creating space for positivity to flourish. Here are some techniques to help you remove negativity from your life.

Heighten Self-Awareness

Cultivate a mindful and introspective approach to your thoughts, emotions, and overall well-being. Pay attention to how different people, situations, and environments make you feel. Notice any patterns of negativity that emerge and the impact they have on your energy levels. No one can know you better than yourself. So, don't let anything go unnoticed by you.

Work on Your Relationships

Having evaluated the quality and impact of your relationships, you must have seen individuals who consistently bring negativity into your life. Do you observe certain interactions that leave you feeling drained, unappreciated, or disempowered? Consider setting boundaries, having open and honest conversations, or, if necessary, gradually distancing yourself from toxic relationships.

Rework Your Thoughts and Beliefs

When you have identified recurring negative thoughts that hinder your well-being. Challenge these negative thoughts and replace them with positive, empowering affirmations. This is where you would begin to harness the power of your mind. There is a profound saying that "a man is controlled by the state of his mind".

Rework Your Media Consumption

Having examined the content you consume regularly, including news, social media, and entertainment, and you have found that they constantly expose you to negative and distressing information; consider limiting your exposure to negative media and seeking positive and uplifting sources instead. This may include games, genre of movie, and music you listen to.

Mindful Detox

Take intentional breaks from technology, particularly social media, to cleanse your mind and reset your energy. Create designated times or spaces for digital detox, allowing yourself to engage in activities that nourish your well-being, such as reading, spending time in nature, or pursuing creative hobbies.

Let Go of Negative Habits

Bad habits are bad; you should not keep them. Once you have identified some negative habits, begin to work at removing them. You can do this by eradicating their triggers and exercising self-control.

Practice Emotional Hygiene

Regularly check in with your emotions and emotional well-being. Allow yourself to acknowledge and process negative emotions rather than suppressing them. Seek healthy outlets for expressing and managing your emotions, such as journaling, talking to a trusted friend or therapist, or engaging in activities that bring you joy.

Cultivate a Positive Support System

Surround yourself with positive and supportive individuals who uplift your energy. Seek out friends, family members, or community groups that foster positivity, encouragement, and growth. Share your journey with like-minded individuals who can provide guidance and support along the way.

Create a Sanctuary

Designate a physical space that promotes positivity and relaxation. Declutter and organise your living and workspace to create a harmonious environment. Incorporate elements that inspire and uplift you, such as plants, meaningful objects, or artwork.

Engage in Self-Care Practices

Prioritise self-care activities that replenish your energy and well-being. This can include practicing mindfulness and meditation, engaging in regular exercise or physical activity, nourishing your body with healthy food, ensuring adequate sleep, and engaging in activities that bring you joy and fulfilment.

Seek Professional Help

If negative energy persists or significantly impacts your daily life, consider seeking support from a therapist, counsellor, or coach. They can provide guidance, tools, and strategies tailored to your specific needs to help you navigate and overcome challenging situations.

Note that the journey of removing negative energy is a continuous process that requires self-reflection, intentionality, and self-compassion. So, be deliberate and consistent.

"Happiness comes from knowing what you truly value and aligning your life accordingly"

– Martin Seligman

BOOSTING POSITIVE ENERGY: TRANSFORMING MINDSETS AND PRACTICES

Cultivating positive energy requires practice and intention. Fortunately, there are powerful techniques we can employ to foster positivity in our daily lives. Mindfulness, as studied by Kabat-Zinn (2003), allows us to be fully present, embracing each moment of acceptance and gratitude. Gratitude journaling, as suggested by Emmons and McCullough (2003), helps us cultivate appreciation for the small blessings in life. Engaging in positive self-talk, as advocated by

Kristin Neff (2011), promotes self-compassion and empowers us to overcome self-doubt.

In our pursuit of cultivating positive energy, it is essential to incorporate techniques that enhance our well-being and nurture a positive mindset. By adopting practices rooted in mindfulness, gratitude, and positive self-talk, we can uplift our spirits, increase our resilience, and invite more positivity into our lives. Let us explore these transformative techniques inspired by the wisdom of renowned positive psychologists.

Embrace Mindfulness

Engage in the present moment with full awareness, allowing yourself to experience life more deeply and appreciatively. Mindfulness practices, such as meditation, breathing exercises, or mindful movement, can help calm the mind, reduce stress, and promote a sense of inner peace. As Dr. Barbara Fredrickson suggests, *"Mindfulness helps you go home to the present. And every time you go there and recognise a condition of happiness that you have, happiness comes."* We will look at this technique closely in later in this book.

Cultivate Gratitude

Develop a gratitude practice by regularly acknowledging and appreciating the blessings and positive aspects of your life. Gratitude is not a feeling of indebtedness to people who do good to you. In that case, you are paying back for something. Gratitude is a thing of your heart. When someone does good to you, you open your heart to receive it. This will change your attitude and open your mind to the good things in the world. Consequently, you will be grateful for live and for people. Sooner you will start rendering help to people without a feeling of getting something back. As Martin Seligman notes, *"Gratitude can transform common days into thanksgivings, turn routine jobs into joy, and change ordinary opportunities into blessings."* We will look at this technique closely in later in this book.

Engage in Positive Self-Talk

Replace self-criticism and negative self-talk with empowering and compassionate inner dialogue. Challenge self-limiting beliefs and replace them with affirmations that inspire confidence, self-acceptance, and resilience. Remember the words of Carol Dweck: *"The view you adopt for yourself profoundly affects the way you lead your life."* We will look at this technique closely in later in this book.

Surround Yourself with Positivity

Seek out inspirational and uplifting content that aligns with your values and aspirations. Surround yourself with books, podcasts, and motivational quotes that foster a positive mindset. Create a vision board or digital collection of images and words that evoke feelings of joy, motivation, and inspiration. As Dacher Keltner suggests, *"Fill your life with things that inspire you."*

Practice Acts of Kindness

Engage in random acts of kindness and compassionate gestures towards others. Helping and supporting others not only generates positive energy within ourselves, but also strengthens social connections and fosters a sense of belonging. As Daniel Kahneman highlights, *"Spending time with people you care about, and who care about you, is one source of happiness."*

Engage in Physical Activity

Incorporate regular physical exercise into your routine to boost your energy levels and promote a sense of well-being. Engaging in activities that get your body moving, such as walking, dancing, or practicing yoga, releases endorphins, which are known to elevate mood and increase positivity.

Seek Meaning and Purpose

Reflect on your values, passions, and aspirations. Engage in activities that align with your sense of purpose and bring meaning to your life. This can involve pursuing hobbies, volunteering, or engaging in work that allows you to make a positive impact. As Dr. Barbara Fredrickson emphasises, *"Engaging in activities that are personally meaningful connects us to something larger than ourselves."*

Foster Positive Relationships

Cultivate supportive and nurturing relationships that uplift your energy and contribute to your well-being. Surround yourself with people who inspire and encourage you to be the best version of yourself. As Carol Dweck advises, *"Surround yourself with people who can help you grow."*

Take Time for Self-Care

Prioritise self-care activities that replenish your physical, mental, and emotional well-being. This can include engaging in activities you enjoy, setting boundaries to protect your energy, practicing relaxation techniques, or seeking professional support when needed. As Dr. Barbara Fredrickson reminds us, *"Self-care is essential for maintaining and replenishing your positive energy reserves."*

Reflect and Celebrate Progress

Take moments to reflect on your journey towards cultivating positive energy. Celebrate your achievements, no matter how small, and acknowledge the growth and progress you have made. As you continue on this path, remember the words of Martin Seligman: *"Happiness is not the absence of negative feelings, but the ability to bounce back from them."*

Incorporating these techniques into your daily life can create a powerful shift in your energy, mindset, and overall well-being. Start with small, actionable steps, and gradually integrate them into your routine. Remember, it is through consistent practice and self-compassion that we can truly harness the transformative power of positive energy. By embracing mindfulness, gratitude, positive self-talk, and other empowering practices, you are actively cultivating the positive energy necessary to lead a more fulfilling and joyful life.

"The science of positive psychology teaches us that happiness and fulfilment come from harnessing our strengths, connecting with others, and living a life of purpose."

— Dacher Keltner

Now, as we venture into the next chapter, we will explore the power of optimism, how to cultivate it, and change our lives. Prepare to embark on a journey of spreading positivity and creating meaningful connections that ripple through the fabric of our lives.

BE DELIBRATE

Creating a culture of positivity is deliberate. You will enjoy the transformative power of positive energy by how much effort you put into it.

2
THE POWER OF OPTIMISM

"Optimism is the faith that leads to achievement. Nothing can be done without hope and confidence".

– Helen Keller

Optimism is a mental attitude that interprets situations and events as hopeful and positive. It is a belief that the future will be better than the present or the past. Optimists tend to expect good things to happen and believe that they can control their own destiny. It is a powerful mindset rooted in positive expectations and a hopeful outlook, holds the key to unlocking a life filled with happiness, resilience, and success. It is the belief that challenges are opportunities for growth, setbacks are temporary, and a bright future awaits. In this chapter, we will explore the profound impact of optimism on our well-being, relationships, and overall quality of life.

Optimism and pessimism are two very different ways of looking at the world. Optimists see the glass as half full, while pessimists see it as half empty. Optimists believe good things will happen, while pessimists believe bad things will happen. To truly understand the essence of optimism, it is essential to distinguish it from mere wishful thinking or blind positivity. Optimism is not about denying the existence of difficulties or disregarding negative emotions (Fredrickson, 2009). Instead, it involves acknowledging the realities of life while maintaining a positive outlook and the belief that one can navigate through adversity and achieve favourable outcomes. Optimism is rooted in the understanding that setbacks and obstacles are part of the human experience, but they do not define our future. It is about reframing negative events as temporary and specific, rather than permanent and all-encompassing. It is a perspective that looks for lessons, growth opportunities, and alternative paths when faced with challenges. An optimistic mindset goes beyond fleeting moments of positivity; it is a way of approaching life consistently. Optimistic individuals tend to focus on their strengths, skills, and past successes, using them as sources of motivation and confidence in the face of new challenges. They embrace a growth mindset, believing in their ability to learn, adapt, and improve.

OPTIMISM IS A HOPEFUL ATTITUDE

Optimism is not about being naïve or overlooking potential risks. It involves a realistic assessment of situations while maintaining a hopeful attitude. It allows individuals to anticipate positive outcomes, even in the face of uncertainty, and take proactive steps towards achieving their goals.

Optimism extends beyond the individual level and influences social interactions. Optimistic individuals radiate positive energy, inspiring and uplifting those around them. Their hopeful outlook fosters resilience, empathy, and a sense of connectedness, creating an environment conducive to growth and positive relationships.

At this, break it down a little to make it clearer here;

ESSENCE OF OPTIMISM

Positive Expectations: Optimism involves having positive expectations about the future. It is the belief that things will work out for the best, even in the face of uncertainty or adversity. Optimistic individuals maintain a hopeful outlook and expect positive outcomes. As Dr. Martin Seligman, the father of positive psychology, stated, *"Optimism is a cognitive bias that leads us to see the world through rose-coloured glasses."* For example, when faced with a challenging project at work, an optimistic person may believe in their ability to overcome obstacles, find innovative solutions, and achieve success. On the other hand, a pessimist will whine and keep complaining because they cannot see any way forward.

Resilience in the Face of Setbacks: Optimism enables individuals to bounce back from setbacks and setbacks. It is the ability to view failures or setbacks as temporary and specific, rather than permanent and all-encompassing. Optimistic individuals see setbacks as opportunities for growth and learning, using them as stepping stones to future success. Psychologist Dr. Carol Dweck, known for her work on growth mindset, states, *"Optimistic people tend to interpret setbacks as temporary, local, and changeable."* For example, an optimist who faces rejection from a job application might view it as a temporary setback, maintaining the belief that the right opportunity will come along and that this rejection does not define their future prospects.

Proactive Problem-Solving: Optimism is closely linked to proactive problem-solving. Optimistic individuals take an active approach to challenges, seeking solutions and opportunities for improvement. They believe in their ability to influence outcomes and take the necessary actions to achieve their goals. Dr. Daniel Kahneman, stated in his book "Thinking, Fast and Slow," that *"Optimism is normal, and it is good for decision-making."* For example, an optimistic person facing financial difficulties may explore various strategies, such as budgeting, seeking additional income sources, or developing new skills to enhance their employability.

DISPELLING MISCONCEPTIONS ABOUT OPTIMISM

Naivety or Ignoring Reality: Optimism should not be confused with naivety or ignoring the realities of life. Optimistic individuals are aware of potential risks and challenges, but choose to focus on the positive aspects and opportunities. They maintain a realistic perspective while nurturing a hopeful outlook. Barbara Fredrickson, in her book "Positivity," explains, *"Optimism is not blind. It's a perspective that focuses on the positive, acknowledges the negative, and seeks to move forward with hope."* For example, an optimistic individual facing a health issue may acknowledge the gravity of the situation, but choose to focus on the treatment options, support systems, and potential for recovery.

Ignoring Negative Emotions: Optimism does not mean suppressing or ignoring negative emotions. Optimistic individuals experience a range of emotions, including sadness, frustration, or disappointment. However, they do not let these emotions define their overall outlook. Instead, they use them as fuel for growth and motivation.

Dacher Keltner, in his book "Born to Be Good," explains, *"Optimism doesn't mean ignoring the negative, but rather embracing a wide range of emotions while maintaining a hopeful perspective."* For example, an optimistic person going through a breakup may allow themselves to feel the pain but also believe that they will heal, learn from the experience.

As we delve into the world of optimism, let us draw inspiration from esteemed positive psychologists, social scientists, and thought leaders who have extensively researched and championed the power of this transformative mindset. Their groundbreaking work has shed light on the numerous benefits of embracing optimism and the practical steps we can take to cultivate it.

Martin Seligman highlights the importance of learned optimism. He argues that by challenging negative beliefs and reframing setbacks as temporary and specific, we can develop a resilient and optimistic perspective. Seligman's research shows that individuals with an optimistic outlook are more likely to overcome adversity, achieve their goals, and experience higher levels of life satisfaction.

Dacher Keltner, a professor of psychology and the director of the Greater Good Science Centre, highlights the social benefits of optimism. His studies reveal optimistic individuals are more likely to build and maintain strong relationships, as their positive energy and belief in a better future are contagious. Optimism fosters empathy, compassion, and a sense of connectedness with others, creating a ripple effect of positivity in our interactions.

"The pessimist sees difficulty in every opportunity. The optimist sees opportunity in every difficulty."

— Winston Churchill

THE BENEFITS OF OPTIMISM

Optimism, with its profound influence on our thoughts, emotions, and actions, brings forth a multitude of benefits that can positively transform our lives. By embracing an optimistic mindset, we open ourselves up to a world of possibilities and experience an array of psychosocial, emotional, and cognitive advantages. Drawing inspiration from esteemed positive psychologists and my personal journey, let us explore the remarkable benefits that optimism can bestow upon us.

Increased Resilience

When faced with adversity, optimism acts as a shield, allowing us to bounce back and recover more quickly. It enables us to reframe challenges as temporary setbacks, providing the motivation and determination to persevere. Personally, I have encountered many hurdles along my path, but through optimism, I have been able to navigate through them with resilience. I echo the sentiment of Martin Seligman, who said, *"Optimism is invaluable for the meaningful life. With a firm belief in a positive future, we can endure hardship and emerge stronger."*

Enhanced Emotional Well-Being

Optimism nurtures a positive emotional state, fostering happiness, contentment, and a greater sense of well-being. By focusing on positive aspects of life and cultivating gratitude, we create a ripple effect of positive emotions. Personally, I have experienced a profound shift in my emotional well-being through the practice of optimism. Even in challenging times, I have found solace in the belief that brighter days lie ahead. As Dr. Barbara Fredrickson affirms, *"Optimism can be cultivated, and by doing so, we increase our daily experiences of positive emotions."*

Improved Physical Health

Research suggests that optimism is linked to better physical health outcomes. Optimistic individuals tend to engage in healthier behaviours, such as regular exercise, balanced nutrition, and adequate sleep. They also demonstrate lower levels of stress, which can positively impact immune function and cardiovascular health. Personally, I have witnessed the transformative effect of optimism on my physical well-being. By maintaining a positive outlook, I have felt more motivated to prioritise self-care, leading to increased vitality and overall health.

Enhanced Relationships

Optimism creates a positive ripple effect in our social interactions. By radiating positive energy, we attract and maintain strong, supportive relationships. Our optimism becomes contagious, inspiring, and uplifting those around us. Personally, I have seen how optimism has enriched my relationships. By approaching interactions with a hopeful mindset, I have fostered deeper connections, empathy, and understanding. I resonate with Dacher Keltner's words: *"Optimism not only makes us feel good, but it also enhances the quality of our relationships, as we become sources of positivity for others."*

Success and Achievement

Optimism fuels a sense of possibility and belief in our abilities, propelling us towards success. By maintaining a positive mindset, we become more likely to set and achieve challenging goals, persist in the face of obstacles, and seize opportunities. Personally, optimism has played a pivotal role in my journey towards success. It has instilled in me the courage to take risks, learn from failures, and embrace new opportunities. I align with Carol Dweck's wisdom: *"With an optimistic mindset, we can unlock our full potential and achieve greatness."*

Through my personal experiences, I have witnessed the profound impact of optimism on my life. It has enabled me to navigate adversity with resilience, maintain a high quality of life, and unlock my true potential. Embracing an optimistic mindset has transformed the way I perceive the world, empowering me to live a life filled with joy, fulfilment, and meaningful connections.

In my personal journey, optimism has played a pivotal role in helping me navigate through various challenges and achieve success in my academic, career, and overall life. Let me share a specific example of how optimism has been a guiding force during a significant academic and career transition.

Many years ago, I found myself at a crossroads in my academic pursuits. I had just completed my undergraduate degree, and although I had dreams of pursuing a particular field of study in graduate school, I faced numerous obstacles. The competition was fierce, and the resources and opportunities seemed limited. Doubt and uncertainty crept into my mind, making me question my abilities and chances of success.

However, instead of succumbing to negativity and self-doubt, I chose to embrace optimism as my guiding light. I firmly believed that setbacks were temporary and that there were alternative paths to achieving my goals. With the inspiration of positive psychologists like Martin Seligman and Carol Dweck, I adopted a growth mindset, viewing challenges as opportunities for personal and intellectual growth.

I embarked on a journey of self-discovery, exploring different avenues related to my field of interest. I reached out to professors, professionals, and alumni who shared similar passions, seeking guidance and mentorship. Through networking and perseverance, I discovered research opportunities, internships, and conferences that allowed me to gain valuable experience and broaden my knowledge.

Despite facing rejection and setbacks along the way, my optimistic outlook fuelled my determination and resilience. I embraced failures as learning opportunities, adjusting my approach, and setting new goals. Each rejection letter or disappointing outcome became a stepping stone toward self-improvement and growth. I held onto the belief that every setback was simply a redirection toward a more fulfilling path.

Eventually, my optimism and perseverance paid off. I received an acceptance letter from a prestigious graduate program that aligned perfectly with my academic and career aspirations. It was a moment of triumph and validation, affirming that optimism, resilience, and a growth mindset were powerful tools in overcoming challenges.

Moreover, this mindset of optimism has continued to shape my career and personal life. It has empowered me to approach new opportunities with enthusiasm, embrace change, and maintain a positive outlook in the face of uncertainty. The lessons learned from my academic journey have translated into other aspects of my life, allowing me to face challenges with resilience, adaptability, and unwavering belief in my ability to overcome obstacles.

My personal experience serves as a testament to the transformative power of optimism. By embracing an optimistic mindset, we can navigate through the toughest of challenges, maintain a sense of hope, and seize opportunities that lead to personal and professional fulfilment. As we start our own paths, let's remember this quote:

"Optimism is a key to success and a pathway to a positive and meaningful life."

– Martin Seligman

As we progress through this journey, let us delve deeper into actionable strategies and practices that can cultivate optimism, allowing us to unlock its transformative power.

HOW TO CULTIVATE OPTIMISM IN YOUR DAILY LIFE

"The only thing that is impossible is the thing you don't try."

– George Bernard Shaw

Optimism is not just an innate trait; it is a skill that can be cultivated and nurtured in our daily lives. By consciously adopting certain practices, we can reframe negative thoughts and train our minds to focus on the positive aspects of life. Let's explore actionable steps to cultivate optimism and embrace its transformative power.

Practice Thought Awareness

Begin by developing an awareness of your thoughts. Notice when negative or pessimistic thoughts arise and consciously redirect your focus. Challenge negative self-talk and replace it with positive affirmations. For example, if you catch yourself thinking, "I'll never be able to do this," reframe it as, "I may face challenges, but I have the ability to overcome them."

Reframe Negative Events

Train yourself to view setbacks or failures as opportunities for growth. Instead of dwelling on what went wrong, focus on the lessons learned and the potential for improvement. Always look for a lesson to learn from everything that comes against you and embrace a growth mindset that sees challenges as stepping stones to success. As Carol Dweck famously said, *"The view you adopt for yourself profoundly affects the way you lead your life."*

Visualise Success

Engage in positive visualisation by imagining yourself successfully overcoming challenges and achieving your goals. Visualise the positive outcomes you desire and feel the emotions associated with that success. This practice not only boosts optimism but also motivates and directs your actions towards your desired outcomes.

Gratitude shifts our focus towards the positive aspects of life. Each day, take a moment to reflect on what you are grateful for, whether it's a loving relationship, a beautiful sunset, or a personal achievement. Expressing gratitude helps rewire our brains to notice and appreciate the good in our lives, enhancing our overall optimism. Surrounding yourself with positive influences can significantly affect your optimism. Seek supportive and optimistic individuals who inspire and uplift you. Engage in activities that bring you joy and foster a positive mindset. Remember, as Martin Seligman stated, *"Optimism is contagious; it can change the course of conversations and relationships."*

In my journey, cultivating optimism has transformed my perspective and outlook on life. By consciously reframing negative thoughts and embracing the power of positivity, I have experienced increased resilience, a greater sense of gratitude, and a renewed belief in my ability to overcome obstacles. As you embark on your own path of cultivating optimism, remember the words of Dacher Keltner: *"Optimism is not just a mental disposition; it's a life practice."* Embrace the power of reframing negative thoughts and focusing on the positive aspects of life. By doing so, you will nurture a resilient and optimistic mindset that propels you toward personal growth, happiness, and success.

SUSTAINING OPTIMISM: PRACTICAL STRATEGIES IN TOUGH TIMES

In challenging times, sustaining optimism can be a powerful tool for navigating through difficulties and maintaining a positive mindset. By adopting practical strategies, individuals can cultivate and sustain optimism even when faced with adversity. Here are some key strategies for sustaining optimism in challenging times:

Cultivating a Positive Mindset

- **Practice Gratitude:** Regularly express gratitude for the positive aspects of your life.

- **Focus on Solutions:** Instead of dwelling on problems, shift your focus to finding solutions.

- **Embrace Positivity:** Surround yourself with positive people, environments, and experiences.

Practicing Self-Care

- **Prioritise Self-care Activities:** Engage in activities that bring you joy and relaxation.

- **Maintain a Healthy Lifestyle:** Exercise regularly, eat nutritious foods, and get enough sleep.

- **Engage in Mindfulness Practices:** Practice meditation, deep breathing, or journaling to centre yourself and reduce stress.

Setting Realistic Goals

- **Break Goals into Smaller, Manageable Steps:** Focus on achievable milestones to maintain motivation.

- **Celebrate Progress:** Acknowledge and celebrate each step forward, no matter how small.

- **Stay Adaptable:** Be open to adjusting your goals and strategies as needed to navigate challenges.

Surrounding Yourself with Support

- **Seek Support from Loved Ones:** Share your concerns and seek guidance from trusted friends and family members.

- **Join a Community:** Engage with groups or organisations that align with your interests and values.

- **Seek Professional Help if Needed:** If you're struggling with maintaining optimism, consider reaching out to a therapist or counsellor.

By incorporating these practical strategies into your life, you can sustain optimism in challenging times and foster a positive outlook. Remember, optimism is a mindset that can be developed and nurtured, and it has the power to transform how you navigate difficulties and embrace the possibilities of the future.

TRIUMPH THROUGH OPTIMISM: PERSONAL STORIES OF OVERCOMING ADVERSITY

"Optimism is the madness of insisting that all is well when we are miserable".

— Voltaire

Optimism has the remarkable ability to help individuals overcome even the most daunting adversities. Let's delve deeper into the inspiring stories of four individuals who defied the odds, using the power of optimism to triumph over their challenges.

Oprah Winfrey

Oprah Winfrey's journey from a difficult upbringing to becoming one of the most influential figures in media is a testament to the power of optimism. Born into poverty in rural Mississippi, Oprah faced a challenging childhood marked by abuse and hardship. However, she held onto a glimmer of hope, believing that her life had a greater purpose. Despite facing setbacks and discrimination, Oprah's unwavering optimism fuelled her determination to succeed. Through hard work, resilience, and an indomitable spirit, Oprah carved a path for herself in the media industry. She became a talk show host, launching "The Oprah Winfrey Show," which went on to become one of the most successful and impactful television programs of all time. Oprah's positive outlook on life, coupled with her commitment to empower and inspire others, led her to establish media companies, philanthropic endeavours, and a platform to uplift countless individuals around the world.

J. K. Rowling

Before the immense success of the Harry Potter series, J.K. Rowling experienced a period of profound adversity. As a single mother living on welfare, she faced financial struggles and the weight of personal setbacks. Additionally, her initial attempts to get her manuscript published were met with rejection after rejection. However, Rowling's optimism remained unshaken. Drawing inspiration from her own experiences and channelling her creative energy, Rowling forged ahead with determination. She transformed her setbacks into stepping stones, using her love for storytelling to craft a captivating world of magic and adventure. Eventually, her persistence paid off when Bloomsbury Publishing recognised the potential of the Harry Potter series.

Rowling's optimism not only led her to achieve remarkable success as an author, but also inspired millions of readers, young and old alike. Through her story, she reminds us that even in the darkest of times, there is always a glimmer of hope, and with resilience and belief in oneself, we can create our own magic.

Nick Vujicic

Born without arms and legs, Nick Vujicic faced immense physical and emotional challenges from an early age. Throughout his childhood, he grappled with feelings of isolation and struggled to find acceptance in a society that often focused on his differences. However, Nick's indomitable spirit and unwavering optimism enabled him to embrace his unique circumstances. Instead of dwelling on his limitations, Nick focused on what he could do rather than what he couldn't. He learned to write, type, swim, and even surf using his foot. Nick refused to let his physical condition define him or hinder his pursuit of a fulfilling life. Embracing his purpose as a motivational speaker, he travelled the world, sharing his story of resilience, hope, and self-acceptance.

Nick's optimism resonated with people from all walks of life, inspiring them to overcome their own challenges and embrace a positive mindset. His message of self-love, gratitude, and perseverance continues to touch the hearts of millions, reminding us that our attitude towards life can triumph over any obstacle.

Nelson Mandela

Nelson Mandela's personal story is one of incredible resilience and optimism. Born in 1918 in South Africa, Mandela grew up in a country plagued by racial segregation and oppression under the apartheid regime. As an anti-apartheid activist, Mandela fought tirelessly for equality and justice. His unwavering optimism became a driving force in his pursuit of a free and democratic South Africa. Despite enduring 27 years of imprisonment, Mandela never lost hope and remained committed to his vision of a united nation.

Upon his release in 1990, Mandela played a pivotal role in dismantling the apartheid system and became South Africa's first black president in 1994.

His leadership and unwavering optimism in the face of immense adversity inspired people around the world. Mandela's personal story serves as a testament to the power of forgiveness, reconciliation, and the belief that a brighter future is possible, even in the most challenging of circumstances.

Stephen Hawking

He was diagnosed with amyotrophic lateral sclerosis (ALS) at the age of 21. ALS is a progressive neurodegenerative disease that affects nerve cells in the brain and spinal cord. It causes muscle weakness and wasting and eventually leads to death. Doctors gave Hawking only a few years to live, but he defied the odds and lived for over 50 years. During that time, he became one of the world's most renowned physicists and authors. He wrote several best-selling books, including A Brief History of Time, which has sold over 10 million copies worldwide.

Hawking's story is an inspiration to us all. It shows us that even in the face of great adversity, we can still achieve great things. Hawking's optimism and determination were essential to his success. He never gave up hope, even when things were tough.

He always believed that he could make a difference in the world.

These extraordinary individuals demonstrate that optimism can serve as a guiding light in even the darkest of times. Their stories remind us that optimism is not simply wishful thinking; it is a mindset that empowers us to persevere, find strength within ourselves, and make a positive impact on the world. We can all learn from Hawking's story. When we are faced with challenges, we should not give up hope. We should choose to be optimistic and believe that we can overcome any obstacle. If we do, we can achieve anything we set our minds to.

Narendra Modi

Narendra Modi, the current Prime Minister of India, his journey is a remarkable example of an individual who has overcome adversity through the power of optimism. Born in 1950 in Vadnagar, Gujarat, Modi faced economic hardships in his early years. However, his unwavering optimism and determination propelled him forward. With a deep interest in spirituality and service, Modi dedicated his life to self-improvement and the pursuit of knowledge.

Despite facing challenges, Modi's optimism remained unshaken. He rose through the ranks of the Rashtriya Swayamsevak Sangh (RSS), a Hindu nationalist organisation, and became actively involved in politics. In 2002, during his tenure as the Chief Minister of Gujarat, the state witnessed communal riots that resulted in widespread violence and loss of life. Despite facing criticism, political conspiracy and false allegations, Modi refused to be deterred. Instead, he recognised the need for change, growth, and reconciliation. He channelled his optimism into transforming Gujarat's economy and infrastructure, attracting investments and fostering inclusive growth. His journey serves as an inspiring reminder that optimism, coupled with resilience and a belief in one's abilities, can help overcome adversity and create meaningful change.

Modi's personal story exemplifies how optimism, resilience, and a steadfast belief in one's abilities can overcome adversity and create meaningful change. His journey inspires millions, demonstrating that determination, hard work, and a positive mindset can transcend circumstances and make a lasting impact on society.

Narendra Modi's story serves as a reminder that optimism, coupled with a commitment to service and progress, can transform both individual lives and the destiny of a nation.

Rosa Parks

Rosa Parks, an iconic figure in the civil rights movement, overcame adversity through the power of optimism. Born in 1913 in Tuskegee, Alabama, Parks grew up in a deeply segregated society. She faced racial discrimination and inequality on a daily basis. However, Parks refused to accept the status quo and believed in the power of change. Her optimism and unwavering belief in justice led her to take a stand against racial segregation on December 1, 1955, when she refused to give up her seat to a white passenger on a bus in Montgomery, Alabama. This act of defiance sparked the Montgomery Bus Boycott and became a pivotal moment in the fight for civil rights. Parks' courage, coupled with her optimism, ignited a movement that would bring about significant change in the United States.

Despite facing threats and challenges, Parks remained steadfast in her belief that equality was attainable. Her resilience and optimism inspired countless individuals and continue to resonate today, reminding us that even in the face of adversity, one person's actions can have a profound impact on society.

Lessons to Learn about Optimism from these Stories

- ⟡ Optimism is a choice. We can choose to be optimistic, even in the face of adversity.

- ⟡ Optimism can help us overcome challenges. When we are optimistic, we are more likely to take risks, try new things, and persevere in the face of setbacks.

- ⟡ Optimism can lead to success. Optimists are more likely to succeed in life. They are healthier and live longer, and they are happier and have more fulfilling relationships.

- ⟡ If you want to overcome adversity and live a more fulfilling life, choose to be optimistic. It won't always be easy, but it will be worth it.

3
THE IMPORTANCE OF SELF-LOVE

"Love yourself first, and everything else falls into line."

– Jean-Jacques Rousseau

In a world that often emphasises external validation and comparison, self-love becomes a vital pillar for cultivating a positive life. It is a profound practice that can revolutionise our lives. It is not about being self-absorbed or selfish, but rather about recognising our inherent value and prioritising our own well-being. At its core, self-love is the deep and unwavering acceptance of oneself. It is a transformative practice that involves embracing our entire being, including our strengths, weaknesses, and imperfections. Carl Rogers, a renowned psychologist, emphasises the importance of self-acceptance, stating that *"The curious paradox is that when I accept myself just as I am, then I can change."* Self-love plays a pivotal role in our personal growth, well-being, and overall happiness. A.P. Gregg and C. Sedikides highlight its significance by stating, *"Self-love is central to psychological health, well-being, and positive functioning."* Here are the key reasons self-love is of utmost importance:

Why is self-love so important? Because it forms the cornerstone of our relationship with ourselves and sets the tone for how we engage with the world. When we love ourselves, we acknowledge our worthiness for joy, fulfilment, and success. We recognise that our needs and desires matter and deserve attention. This acknowledgment fuels a positive cycle of self-empowerment and self-care, leading to a greater sense of well-being and a more fulfilling life.

THE BENEFITS OF SELF-LOVE

"Talk to yourself like someone you love."

– Brene Brown

Self-love, with its profound impact on our well-being and relationships, holds a multitude of benefits that enrich our lives and create a ripple effect of positivity and love in the world. As we draw inspiration from esteemed authors and psychologists, we embark on a journey that unveils the transformative power of self-love.

Increased Confidence

When we embrace self-love, our confidence soars. We develop a deep sense of self-worth and acceptance, allowing us to stand tall in our own uniqueness. As Carol Dweck states, *"Believing in yourself is crucial. You have to believe that you are capable of achieving anything you set your mind to."* With self-love as our foundation, we step into the world with a newfound confidence, ready to tackle challenges and pursue our dreams.

Enhanced Relationships

Self-love forms the bedrock for healthy, fulfilling relationships. By honouring our own needs and setting boundaries, we establish a framework for authentic connections. When we love ourselves, we attract and cultivate relationships that reflect our self-worth. We will be able to block negative influences from reaching our personal space. As Oprah Winfrey beautifully puts it, *"You get in life what you have the courage to ask for."* Through self-love, we learn to ask for and receive the love and respect we deserve.

Emotional Resilience

Self-love equips us with the emotional resilience needed to navigate life's ups and downs. As we cultivate a deep well of self-compassion, we become more adept at handling setbacks and challenges. Abraham Maslow, renowned for his work on human motivation, reminds us, *"What is necessary to change a person is to change their awareness of themselves."* Through self-love, we shift our awareness, embracing our inherent strength and capacity to overcome obstacles.

Inner Peace and Well-Being

Self-love nurtures our inner peace and well-being. When we prioritise self-care and make space for our needs, we create a harmonious balance in our lives. Rollo May, a renowned existential psychologist, once said, *"The opposite of courage in our society is not cowardice, it is conformity."* Self-love empowers us to break free from societal expectations and embrace a life aligned with our true selves, leading to greater fulfilment and contentment.

Spreading Love and Positivity

The power of self-love extends far beyond ourselves. Just as a stone creates ripples in a pond, our self-love radiates outward, impacting our relationships and the world at large. By embracing self-love, we raise our vibrational frequency, attracting and spreading love, compassion, and positivity. Erich Fromm, a prominent social psychologist, reminds us, *"Love is a decision, it is a judgment, it is a promise. If love were only a feeling, there would be no basis for the promise to love each other forever."*

In my personal journey, self-love has been a transformative force. Through self-reflection, self-care practices, and a commitment to honouring my needs, I have experienced a profound shift in my well-being and relationships. By embracing self-love, I have learned to celebrate my strengths, embrace my imperfections, and treat myself with kindness and compassion. This journey has not only brought me inner peace and happiness, but has also positively influenced the way I engage with others.

As we explore the benefits of self-love, let us remember the profound impact it has on our lives. It empowers us to embrace our uniqueness, nurture fulfilling relationships, cultivate emotional resilience, find inner peace, and spread love and positivity in the world. Jean-Jacques Rousseau once said, *"Love yourself first, and everything else falls into line."* Embrace the transformative power of self-love, and witness how it unfolds a world of possibilities for you and those around you.

SELF-LOVE IS NOT SELFISHNESS

Self-love is not selfishness. It is you having the same compassion you have for others on your own self. If you love yourself, it will be easy for you to love others. Self-love involves taking care of your soul, mind, body, and environment. Knowing that you also deserve the good things of life.

HOW TO CULTIVATE SELF-LOVE IN YOUR DAILY LIFE

"Love yourself. Be clear on how you want to be treated. Know your worth"

– Maryam Hasnaa

In the pursuit of self-love, we embark on a transformative journey that requires nurturing, self-compassion, and intentional practices. The steps have helped me a lot to cultivate self-love in my daily life. Pay good attention to them because through these powerful tips, we create a foundation of love and acceptance that radiates into our relationships and the world.

Practice Self-Compassion

Cultivating self-love begins with showing ourselves kindness and compassion. Understand that you are deserving of love and understanding, just like anyone else. As Denise Francis, a renowned psychologist, reminds us, *"Be gentle with yourself, you're doing the best you can."* Embrace self-compassion by offering yourself forgiveness, understanding, and support, especially during challenging times.

Embrace Self-Care

Prioritising self-care is an essential aspect of cultivating self-love. Carve out time in your daily routine for activities that nourish your mind, body, and soul. Engage in activities that bring you joy, such as practicing mindfulness, engaging in hobbies, or indulging in self-care rituals. Remember Oprah Winfrey's wise words, *"The more you love yourself, the better you are at loving others."*

Set Boundaries

Setting boundaries is a powerful act of self-love. Recognise and honour your limits, both in relationships and in your personal life. Learn to say 'no' when necessary, without guilt or fear of disappointing others. By setting healthy boundaries, you create a space that fosters self-respect, authenticity, and emotional well-being.

Challenge Self-Critical Thoughts

Self-love involves nurturing a positive mindset and challenging self-critical thoughts. Replace self-judgment with self-compassionate and empowering affirmations. As Carol Dweck, a leading researcher in motivation and mindset, suggests, *"Embrace failure as a stepping stone to success. Learn from your mistakes and grow."* Embrace a growth mindset that celebrates progress rather than perfection.

Practice Mindful Self-Reflection

Engage in regular self-reflection to deepen your self-awareness and understanding. Set aside time to check in with yourself, exploring your thoughts, emotions, and needs. Journaling, meditation, or seeking professional guidance can help facilitate this process. As Carl Rogers, a renowned psychologist, stated, *"The curious paradox is that when I accept myself just as I am, then I can change."*

In my personal journey of cultivating self-love, I have found these practices to be transformative. By embracing self-compassion, engaging in self-care, setting boundaries, challenging self-critical thoughts, practicing gratitude, surrounding myself with positivity, and engaging in mindful self-reflection, I have experienced a profound shift in my relationship with myself.

Cultivating self-love has significant benefits for us and the world. When we love ourselves, we will inspire others to do the same. This will create a chain of positive energy that will draw more positivity to our world. So, let us embrace these practices with empathy, knowing that the journey of self-love is a continuous and rewarding one. As Jean-Jacques Rousseau wisely said, *"Love yourself first, and everything else falls into line."*

EMBRACING IMPERFECTIONS: EMPHASISING SELF-ACCEPTANCE AND GROWTH

In a world that often values perfection and places unrealistic expectations on individuals, embracing imperfections becomes an essential aspect of self-love. Emphasising self-acceptance and growth allows us to recognise that imperfections are a natural part of being human. It is through embracing our imperfections that we can cultivate a deeper sense of self-love and nurture personal growth. This topic explores the significance of embracing imperfections and highlights the benefits it brings to our lives.

Embracing Imperfections fosters Self-Acceptance: By acknowledging and accepting our flaws, we can develop a greater sense of self-compassion and self-acceptance. It allows us to release the burden of perfectionism and embrace ourselves as whole individuals, with both strengths and weaknesses.

Emphasising Growth Mindset: Embracing imperfections involves adopting a growth mindset where challenges and setbacks are seen as opportunities for learning and personal development. It encourages us to view mistakes as stepping stones rather than failures, leading to increased resilience and a willingness to take risks.

Cultivating Self-Compassion: Embracing imperfections requires self-compassion, which involves treating ourselves with kindness, understanding, and empathy. It means acknowledging that we are all imperfect and deserving of love and acceptance, including ourselves.

Finding Beauty in Uniqueness: Embracing imperfections allows us to celebrate our uniqueness and recognise that it is our differences that make us special. It encourages us to appreciate the beauty in our individuality and to embrace our authentic selves.

Encouraging Personal Growth: Embracing imperfections creates space for personal growth and transformation. It opens doors to self-exploration, self-improvement, and new possibilities, as we are no longer held back by the fear of making mistakes or not meeting unrealistic standards.

Embracing imperfections and emphasising self-acceptance and growth is a powerful practice that can lead to a more fulfilling and compassionate relationship with ourselves. It allows us to let go of self-judgment, embrace our uniqueness, and embark on a journey of personal growth and self-discovery. By recognising the beauty in imperfections, we create a nurturing environment for self-love to flourish and inspire others to do the same.

SELF-LOVE TRANSFORMATIONS: PERSONAL STORIES OF CHANGE

Throughout history, many individuals have embarked on transformative journeys of self-love, overcoming personal struggles, and emerging as beacons of inspiration. Here are a few of them.

Michelle Obama: Embracing Worthiness and Self-Love

Michelle Obama, the epitome of grace and resilience, has not only left an indelible mark as a former First Lady, but has also become an advocate for self-love and empowerment. In her book, "Becoming," she vulnerably shares her journey towards embracing self-love, inviting readers to accompany her on a path of growth.

For years, Michelle Obama grappled with her self-image and weight, succumbing to society's unrealistic standards. However, she ultimately realised that her worthiness was not defined by appearances or external validation. Michelle Obama's story resonates deeply with countless individuals who have faced similar struggles.

Through her words, she inspires us to recognise our inherent value and embrace self-love unconditionally. Michelle Obama's transformation serves as a testament to the power of embracing one's authentic self and fostering a loving relationship with oneself.

"The journey to self-love is a lifelong one, but it is one of the most important journeys we can take."

— Michelle Obama

Michelle Obama's quote reminds us that self-love is not a destination but a continuous journey. It encourages us to embark on this transformative path and highlights the significance of cultivating self-love in our lives.

Demi Lovato: Embracing Imperfections and Resilience

Demi Lovato is a popular singer and actress who has been candid about her battles with self-love, addiction, and mental health. Her story exemplifies the remarkable strength and resilience

The importance of Self-Love

that can emerge from embracing imperfections and practicing self-compassion.

Lovato's journey to self-love has been marked by moments of self-reflection, acceptance, and learning from her past. She emphasises the importance of being kind to oneself, even when faced with setbacks or mistakes. Demi Lovato's story resonates with individuals grappling with self-doubt, reminding us that self-love is a transformative and ongoing process. Her words and experiences offer solace and motivation to those navigating their own journey of self-love. Demi Lovato serves as a powerful reminder that our flaws do not define us and that we have the capacity to rise above our challenges through self-acceptance and love.

"The most important thing is to accept yourself for who you are and not try to be someone you're not."

— Demi Lovato

Demi Lovato's quote serves as a powerful reminder to embrace our authentic selves. It encourages us to let go of societal expectations and celebrate our unique qualities, fostering self-love rooted in acceptance and authenticity.

These personal stories of transformation through self-love serve as beacons of hope and inspiration. They remind us we are all deserving of love, compassion, and acceptance, regardless of our perceived flaws or past struggles. May their journeys ignite the fire of self-love within us and inspire us to embark on our own transformative paths. Remember, the power to love ourselves unconditionally lies within each of us.

The importance of Self-Love

4
THE ROLE OF MINDFULNESS

"The present moment is the only moment available to us, and it is the door to all moments."

— Thich Nhat Hanh

In our fast-paced and hectic lives, finding moments of calm and inner peace can feel like a distant dream. Nevertheless, we can tap into a wellspring of positive energy that resides within us by the practice of mindfulness. Mindfulness has become a buzzword in recent years, but its significance goes far beyond a passing trend. It is a powerful practice that can transform our lives and increase positive energy. At its core, mindfulness is the art of being fully present in the present moment, without judgment or attachment. It involves paying attention to our thoughts,

The Role of Mindfulness

feelings, and sensations in a non-reactive manner. This allows us to develop a deep sense of awareness and connection to the present moment, ourselves, and the world around us. This enables us to be able to tap into our inner resources and enhance our overall well-being. It involves fully immersing ourselves in our experiences, thoughts, and emotions as they arise, without getting caught up in the past or future. The power of cultivating a non-judgmental awareness of our present-moment experiences, we can unlock the transformative power of mindfulness. Thich Nhat Hanh, a renowned Buddhist monk and author of "The Miracle of Mindfulness," beautifully captures the essence of mindfulness. He states, "*Mindfulness shows us what is happening in our bodies, our emotions, our minds, and in the world. Through mindfulness, we avoid harming ourselves and others.*"

The importance of mindfulness goes into the fact that it can increase positive energy by allowing us to cultivate a deeper sense of gratitude, compassion, and self-acceptance. When we are fully present in each moment, we become attuned to the beauty and wonders that surround us. We develop a heightened appreciation for the simple joys of life, such as the warmth of sunlight on our skin or the melody of birdsong. This awareness nurtures a sense of gratitude within us, uplifting our spirits and infusing our lives with positive energy. Mindfulness nurtures compassion, both towards ourselves and others. As we cultivate a non-judgmental awareness of our thoughts and emotions, we develop greater understanding and empathy. We become more attuned to the needs and struggles of those around us, fostering deeper connections and more meaningful relationships. This compassionate outlook allows positive energy to flow freely, radiating love and kindness into the world. Christopher Germer and Kristin Neff, authors of "The Mindful Path to Self-Compassion," highlight the transformative power of mindfulness in cultivating self-compassion. They write, *"Mindfulness is not meant to erase our difficulties; rather, it offers us a new way of relating to our challenges with kindness, curiosity, and acceptance."*

One major challenge of the digital age is the mental overload we often face. We jump from Twitter to Facebook, and to YouTube without being mindful of what we are doing. More often, we spend a lot of time scrolling and consuming contents on the media. Eventually, we cannot pay enough attention to things that matter in our lives. Mindfulness offers us a respite from the constant busyness and distractions of the digital age. In his book "The

Mindful Geek," Chade-Meng Tan explores how mindfulness can help us find focus and resilience in the face of digital overload. By consciously directing our attention to the present moment, we can reclaim our mental space, reduce stress, and increase our capacity to engage with the world in a meaningful way.

Moreover, mindfulness extends beyond our individual selves and has a ripple effect on our relationships and the world around us. When we cultivate a state of mindfulness, we become more attuned to the needs and emotions of others. We listen deeply, speak with kindness, and foster genuine connections. Our presence and positive energy to create a supportive and nurturing environment, benefiting both ourselves and those around us. In the words of Oprah Winfrey, *"The more you praise and celebrate your life, the more there is in life to celebrate."* By embracing mindfulness, we shift our focus from dwelling on past regrets or anxieties about the future to fully experiencing and appreciating the present moment. This shift in perspective allows us to savour life's joys, find gratitude in even the smallest moments, and cultivate a deep sense of contentment.

It is important to remember that it is a practice—a continuous exploration of our inner landscape. It is not about achieving perfection or escaping from challenges; rather, it is about embracing the richness of our human experience with openness and compassion.

THE BENEFITS OF MINDFULNESS

"The present moment is filled with joy and happiness. If you are attentive, you will see it."

— Thich Nhat Hanh

Mindfulness is a practice that holds a multitude of important benefits, transforming not only our individual lives but also our relationships and overall well-being. Here are some of it.

Reduced Stress

One of the most prominent benefits of mindfulness is its ability to reduce stress. In our fast-paced and demanding lives, stress has become all too common. However, mindfulness offers us a refuge—a space to pause, breathe, and reconnect with the present moment. Research conducted by Barbara Fredrickson and other psychologists reveals that regular mindfulness practice leads to decreased levels of stress hormones and an increased sense of calm and well-being (tang et al., 2015).

Enhanced Focus and Attention

In today's world of constant distractions, cultivating the ability to be fully present and attentive is invaluable. Jon Kabat-Zinn explains in his book that through mindfulness, we develop the capacity to direct our attention intentionally and sustain it, improving our concentration and productivity in various aspects of life.

Heightened Intuition

Heightened intuition is another remarkable benefit of mindfulness. By quieting the mind and tuning in to our inner wisdom, we become more attuned to our instincts and inner guidance. This heightened intuition allows us to make decisions that align with our authentic selves and navigate life's challenges with greater clarity. As Carl Rogers stated, *"The only reality I have is my own intuitive sense of where I am coming from."*

Spiritual Growth

Spiritual growth is also nurtured through mindfulness. While mindfulness is often associated with secular practices, it has deep roots in ancient spiritual traditions. By cultivating a state of mindfulness, we open ourselves to a greater sense of connection with something beyond ourselves. This connection to the transcendent can deepen our understanding of the world and foster a sense of purpose and meaning in our lives.

Enhanced Emotional Intelligence

This is a vital aspect of our interpersonal relationships. As we become more attuned to our own thoughts, feelings, and sensations, we develop a heightened awareness of the emotional experiences of others. This empathic understanding strengthens our ability to communicate, empathise, and build deeper connections with those around us.

Improved Sleep

Improved sleep is yet another benefit of mindfulness. In a world filled with constant stimulation and information overload, many struggle with insomnia and restless nights. Mindfulness practices, such as relaxation techniques and guided meditations, promote a state of relaxation and help us let go of racing thoughts, enabling us to experience restful and rejuvenating sleep.

Increased Self-Awareness

Increased self-awareness is a cornerstone of mindfulness. By turning our attention inward and observing our thoughts, emotions, and bodily sensations, we gain valuable insights into our patterns, habits, and automatic reactions. This self-awareness empowers us to make conscious choices and break free from harmful cycles that no longer serve us.

Better Decision-Making Process

Mindfulness also cultivates better decision-making. When we practise mindfulness, we create space for discernment and clarity. By observing our thoughts and emotions without judgment, we can make decisions from a place of wisdom and intuition rather than being swayed by external pressures or reactive impulses. As Oprah Winfrey wisely states, *"You have to know what sparks the light in you so that you, in your own way, can illuminate the world."*

Patience

Patience is an invaluable quality in today's instant-gratification culture. By practicing mindfulness, we learn to embrace the present moment and accept things as they are, even when they don't align with our expectations. This patience allows us to navigate challenges with grace, understanding that growth and transformation take time.

In living a positive life, mindfulness is key to of living fully in the present moment, savouring the simple joys that surround us. Rolf Potts, in "The Mindful Traveler," explores how mindfulness can be applied to the art of travel, transforming it into a journey of self-discovery and inner growth. Through mindful exploration, we learn to appreciate the beauty and diversity of the world while deepening our connection with ourselves and others. Therefore, we ought to embrace mindfulness as a natural state of being, reminding us we have the capacity to find peace and presence in even the simplest moments. By embracing mindfulness, we embark on a journey of self-exploration and growth. We awaken to the beauty of the present moment, nourish our inner landscapes, and cultivate a deeper understanding of ourselves and the world around us. Mindfulness becomes a guiding light, illuminating our path towards a more peaceful, purposeful, and fulfilling existence. In the words of Oprah Winfrey, *"Breathe. Let go. And remind yourself that this very moment is the only one you know you have for sure."* Through the practice of mindfulness, we open ourselves to the richness of each passing moment, harnessing its potential to transform our lives from within.

MINDFULNESS OPENS UP YOUR INNER-SELF

Mindfulness is a powerful tool that can be used to overcome many challenges in life. If you are struggling with anxiety, depression, stress, or other mental health issues, mindfulness may be a helpful addition to your treatment plan. Mindfulness is not being lost in thought, but actively processing things. Process your thoughts, emotions, actions, and things going on around you. So, take a deep breath, anchor yourself in the present moment, and embark on the remarkable journey of positive living through mindfulness.

TECHNIQUES FOR PRACTICING MINDFULNESS

"Mindfulness means paying attention in a particular way: on purpose, in the present moment, and non-judgementally."

— Jon Kabat-Zinn

Mindfulness has vast benefits, as seen above. In this section, we will look at sustainable ways of practicing mindfulness in our daily living. This will save us from the chaotic living that comes with our fast-paced world.

Mindful Breathing

Begin by finding a comfortable position and bringing your attention to your breath. Notice the natural rhythm of your inhalations and exhalations. Take slow, deep breaths, feeling the gentle rise and fall of your abdomen. Consciously anchoring yourself in the present moment through focused breathing can bring a sense of calm and centeredness to your being.

Body Scan Meditation

Find a quiet space where you can lie down comfortably. Starting from the top of your head, slowly direct your attention to each part of your body, scanning for any sensations or areas of tension. Notice without judgment and allow yourself to release any accumulated stress or discomfort. This practice, inspired by Jon Kabat-Zinn's work in "Wherever You Go, There You Are," cultivates self-awareness and helps foster a deeper connection with your physical being.

Loving-Kindness Meditation

Sit in a relaxed position, bringing to mind someone you care deeply about. Repeat phrases such as, *"May you be happy. May you be healthy. May you be safe. May you live with ease."* Extend these wishes of love and compassion to yourself, loved ones, and eventually to all beings. This practice will help us nurture empathy and expand our capacity for kindness.

Mindful Eating

Transform a simple act into a mindful ritual. Before you start eating, take a moment to observe the colours, textures, and aromas of your food. Engage all your senses as you take each bite, savouring the flavours and appreciating the nourishment it provides. By cultivating awareness during meals, as recommended in Rolf Potts, you can enhance your relationship with food and develop a greater sense of gratitude for the sustenance it offers.

Walking Meditation

Find a peaceful outdoor setting and start walking slowly, paying attention to each step. Feel the sensation of your feet connecting with the ground, the movement of your legs, and the gentle sway of your body. Engage your senses fully, taking in the sights, sounds, and smells of your surroundings. As you walk, let go of distractions and immerse yourself in the present moment. This walking meditation fosters a deep connection with nature and cultivates a sense of groundedness.

Mindful Listening

In our fast-paced world, active and attentive listening is a precious gift we can offer to others. When engaging in conversations, practice truly hearing and understanding the words, emotions, and nuances being expressed. As you listen, refrain from interrupting or formulating your response. Instead, create space for the speaker to share fully. By practicing mindful listening, as highlighted in the works of influential psychologists such as Carl Rogers, you foster deeper connections and cultivate empathy.

Mindful Technology Use

In today's digital age, technology often consumes a significant part of our lives. However, by bringing mindfulness to our interactions with technology, we can find balance and limit distractions. Set aside dedicated time for uninterrupted activities, such as reading, engaging in hobbies, or spending quality time with loved ones. Additionally, establish mindful technology habits, such as turning off notifications, practicing digital detoxes, and setting boundaries to ensure technology serves us rather than dominates us. Chade-Meng Tan's "The Mindful Geek" offers valuable insights into integrating mindfulness into our digital lives.

Mindful Communication

Engage in conscious and mindful communication by pausing before responding, speaking from a place of compassion and understanding, and truly listening to others' perspectives. Allow your words to be thoughtful, kind, and inclusive. This practice, influenced by the principles of Nonviolent Communication and positive psychology, promotes harmony and fosters meaningful connections.

Mindful Reflection

Set aside a dedicated time for self-reflection and introspection. This can take the form of journaling, meditation, or engaging in activities that encourage self-discovery, such as creative expression or spending time in nature. By regularly checking in with yourself, you deepen your self-awareness, gain insights into your thoughts and emotions, and cultivate a sense of inner balance and growth. This technique empowers us to navigate the ebbs and flows of life with grace, resilience, and a deep sense of inner peace.

MINDFULNESS JOURNEYS: STORIES OF PEACE AND CLARITY

"You can't stop the waves, but you can learn to surf."

— Jon Kabat-Zinn

Ellen DeGeneres

Ellen DeGeneres is a comedian, actress, and talk show host who has been open about her struggles with anxiety and depression. She has said that mindfulness has helped her to manage her mental health and live a more present and joyful life. "*Mindfulness has changed my life,* "DeGeneres said in an interview with Oprah Winfrey. *"It's helped me to be more present in the moment and to not worry about the past or the future. It's also helped me to be more compassionate towards myself and others.*" DeGeneres has incorporated mindfulness into her daily routine by practicing meditation and yoga. She also encourages her fans to try mindfulness techniques, such as mindful breathing and body scans.

Arianna Huffington

Arianna Huffington is a businesswoman, author, and former editor-in-chief of The Huffington Post. She has written extensively about the importance of sleep and mindfulness for personal and professional success. *"Mindfulness is the practice of paying attention to the present moment without judgment",* Huffington said in an interview with The New York Times. *"It's a powerful tool that can help us reduce stress, improve our focus and concentration, and make better decisions."* Huffington has incorporated mindfulness into her daily routine by practicing meditation and yoga. She also encourages her readers to try mindfulness techniques, such as mindful eating and walking meditation.

Lessons to Learn from these Individuals

Ellen DeGeneres and Arianna Huffington both used mindfulness to overcome challenges in their lives. Here are some examples of how they did this:

✧ Ellen DeGeneres used mindfulness to manage her anxiety and depression. She found that by practicing meditation and yoga; she was able to calm her mind and body and reduce her stress levels. This helped her to feel more in control of her emotions and to cope better with difficult situations.

✧ Arianna Huffington used mindfulness to improve her sleep. She found that by practicing meditation before bed; she was able to relax her mind and body and fall asleep more easily. This helped her to feel more rested and energised during the day.

✧ Both Ellen DeGeneres and Arianna Huffington used mindfulness to improve their focus and concentration. They found that by practicing meditation; they were able to train their minds to focus on the present moment and to avoid getting distracted. This helped them to be more productive at work and to enjoy their leisure time more fully.

5
GRATITUDE AND POSITIVE SELF-TALK

"Gratitude is the healthiest of all human emotions. The more you express gratitude for what you have, the more likely you will have even more to express gratitude for."

— Ralph Waldo Emerson

Gratitude and positive self-talk are powerful practices that can transform our mindset, enhance our well-being, and cultivate positive energy in our lives. In this chapter, we will explore what gratitude and positive self-talk are, what they are not, and provide examples and illustrations to understand these concepts better.

Gratitude and Positive Self-Talk

Gratitude is the act of acknowledging and appreciating the good things in our lives, both big and small. It involves shifting our focus from what is lacking to what is present, fostering a mindset of abundance and positivity. Gratitude is not about ignoring life's challenges or denying negative emotions; instead, it is about finding the silver linings and recognising the blessings amidst the difficulties. For example, when you are coming home after a long, tiring day at work. Instead of dwelling on the stress and exhaustion, practicing gratitude involves recognising and being thankful for having a supportive family, a comfortable home, or the opportunity to pursue a fulfilling career. It is about shifting our perspective and finding reasons to be grateful in every situation.

Positive self-talk, on the other hand, refers to the internal dialogue we have with ourselves. It involves consciously choosing to focus on affirming and empowering statements that uplift our spirits and foster self-belief. Positive self-talk is not about deluding ourselves with unrealistic positivity or dismissing our genuine struggles; instead, it is about cultivating self-compassion, self-encouragement, and a growth-oriented mindset. For instance, suppose you make a mistake at work. Instead of berating yourself with negative self-talk like "I'm so stupid" or "I'll never succeed," positive self-talk involves reframing the situation with statements like "Mistakes happen, and I can learn from this experience" or "I have the skills and resilience to overcome challenges." It is about nurturing a kind and supportive inner voice that motivates us to keep moving forward.

Gratitude and positive self-talk are essential ingredients for cultivating and sustaining positive energy in our lives. By expressing gratitude, we shift our perspective from negativity to appreciation, allowing us to find joy in the present moment and open ourselves to new opportunities. Scientific studies have shown that gratitude exercises, such as keeping a gratitude journal or expressing gratitude to others, can increase happiness and life satisfaction (Seligman et al., 2005). Gratitude acts as a powerful antidote to negative emotions and helps us reframe challenging situations in a more positive light.

Positive self-talk compliments gratitude by shaping our beliefs and influencing our actions. When we engage in positive self-talk, we replace self-doubt and self-criticism with self-compassion and self-encouragement. This internal dialogue strengthens our confidence, resilience, and motivation to pursue our goals. Psychologist Barbara Fredrickson's broaden-and-build theory suggests that positive emotions, such as gratitude and self-belief, broaden our perspectives and enhance our problem-solving abilities (Fredrickson, 2001). By cultivating gratitude and engaging in positive self-talk, we create a positive feedback loop that fosters personal growth, well-being, and an optimistic outlook on life.

"The more you practice positive self-talk, the more you will believe in yourself and the more likely you are to achieve your goals."

— Steve Maraboli

Through the practice of gratitude and positive self-talk, we can experience profound shifts in our outlook and overall well-being. Cultivating gratitude allows us to find joy in the present moment, appreciate the goodness in our lives, and reframe challenging situations in a more positive light. Positive self-talk empowers us to believe in ourselves, boosts our confidence, and fuels our motivation to pursue our goals. Imagine starting each day by expressing gratitude for the opportunities ahead and affirming your strengths and abilities through positive self-talk. This combination sets the tone for a positive mindset, propelling you towards a more fulfilling and meaningful life.

GRATITUDE AND POSITIVE SELF-TALK IS NOT TEMPORARY

Gratitude and positive self-talk are not just fleeting moments of positivity; they are transformative practices that shape our mindset, influence our emotions, and drive our actions. They allow us to cultivate a positive energy that radiates into all areas of our lives, benefiting our relationships, work, and overall well-being. Cultivating these habits can create a lot of positivity in our lives, those of others.

THE SCIENCE OF GRATITUDE: EXPLORING PSYCHOLOGICAL AND PHYSICAL BENEFITS

This topic explores the empirical evidence behind the power of gratitude. It delves into the scientific research that supports the transformative effects of gratitude on our mental and physical well-being. By examining psychological studies and physiological findings, we gain a deeper understanding of how gratitude rewires our brain, influences our emotions, and impacts our overall health. We uncover the neurological processes involved in experiencing and expressing gratitude, highlighting its ability to shift our perspectives and enhance our sense of well-being. Additionally, we explore the connections between gratitude and stress reduction, resilience, relationships, and even our immune system. This topic offers a comprehensive exploration of the science-backed benefits of gratitude, providing a solid foundation for incorporating gratitude practices into our daily lives.

Here are some key insights and findings:

Rewiring the Brain

- Studies show that gratitude activates neural pathways associated with reward, empathy, and positive emotions.

- Regular gratitude practice can lead to long-lasting changes in brain structure, promoting greater emotional resilience and happiness.

Boosting Psychological Well-Being

- Gratitude is linked to lower levels of depression, anxiety, and stress.

- It enhances overall life satisfaction and positive emotions, fostering a sense of contentment and fulfilment.

Strengthening Relationships

- Expressing gratitude cultivates stronger interpersonal connections and enhances relationship satisfaction.

- Grateful individuals tend to experience higher levels of empathy, compassion, and forgiveness.

Promoting Physical Health

- Gratitude has been associated with better sleep quality and duration, leading to improved overall health.

- It is linked to a stronger immune system, reduced inflammation, and lower blood pressure.

Resilience and Coping

- Gratitude practices help individuals develop resilience, enabling them to navigate adversity and bounce back from challenges.

- It fosters a more optimistic mindset and facilitates adaptive coping strategies.

Enhancing Mental Strength

- Gratitude encourages a shift in focus from negative rumination to positive aspects of life, promoting a healthier mindset.

- It helps individuals develop self-compassion and self-esteem, supporting their overall psychological well-being.

By understanding the science behind gratitude, we can harness its potential to transform our lives. Gratitude practises can foster a more positive mindset, strengthen relationships, and boost our health. The scientific evidence presented in this chapter underscores the significance of gratitude as a powerful tool for enhancing our psychological and physical resilience, ultimately leading to a more fulfilling and joyful life.

TECHNIQUES FOR PRACTISING GRATITUDE

"When you focus on what you have, you'll always have more. When you focus on what you don't have, you'll never ever have enough."

– Oprah Winfrey

Gratitude is a powerful emotion that has been shown to have several benefits for our mental and physical health. When we practise gratitude, we focus on the good things in our lives, and this can help us feel happier, more optimistic, and more resilient.

There are many ways to practise gratitude. Here are a few techniques that you can try:

Keep a Gratitude Journal

This is one of the most popular ways to practise gratitude. Each day, take a few minutes to write three things that you are grateful for. It can be anything, big or small, from the people in your life to the beautiful scenery around you.

Express Gratitude to Others

Another great way to practise gratitude is to express it to others. We can do this in several ways, such as writing a thank-you note, sending a text message, or simply saying "thank you" in person. Meditate on gratitude. Meditation is a powerful tool that can help us focus on the present moment and to appreciate the good things in our lives. There are many ways to meditate on gratitude. One simple way is to sit quietly and focus on your breath. As you breathe in, think about something that you are grateful for. As you breathe out, let go of any negative thoughts or feelings.

Practice Random Acts of Kindness

When we do something kind to someone else, it not only makes them feel good, but it also makes us feel good. This is because helping others activates the same reward centres in our brains that are activated when we experience pleasure.

Be Mindful of Your Thoughts

One of the best ways to increase gratitude is to be mindful of your thoughts. When you catch yourself thinking negative thoughts, challenge them. Ask yourself if there is any evidence to support your negative thoughts. If there is not, then try to replace your negative thoughts with more positive ones.

Focus on the Present Moment

When we focus on the present moment, we are more likely to appreciate the good things in our lives. This is because when we are focused on the past or the future, we are more likely to be thinking about things that we don't have or that we want.

Be Grateful for the Challenges

Challenges can be a source of growth and learning. When we are grateful for the challenges in our lives, we are more likely to see them as opportunities to learn and grow.

Gratitude is a powerful emotion that can have a positive impact on our mental and physical health. By practicing gratitude, we can improve our mood, reduce stress, boost our immune system, and increase our overall well-being.

TECHNIQUES FOR PRACTICING POSITIVE SELF-TALK

"The way you talk to yourself matters. Be kind."

– Brené Brown

Positive self-talk is the practice of talking to yourself in a positive and encouraging way. It can be a powerful tool for improving your mood, increasing your confidence, and achieving your goals.

Here are some techniques for practicing positive self-talk:

Affirmations

Affirmations are positive statements that you repeat to yourself on a regular basis. They can help you to change your negative self-talk and to develop a more positive outlook on life.

When choosing affirmations, it is important to choose statements that are specific, believable, and positive. For example, instead of saying "I am a good person," you might say, "I am kind, compassionate, and helpful."

You can write your affirmations down and read them to yourself, or you can say them out loud. It is also helpful to visualise yourself achieving the goal that your affirmation is about.

Reframing Negative Thoughts

When you have a negative thought, try to reframe it in a more positive way. For example, if you think "I'm not good enough," you might reframe it as "I'm still learning and growing."

It can also be helpful to ask yourself, "What's the worst that could happen?" If you realise that the worst-case scenario is not actually that bad, it can help you feel less anxious and more confident.

Be Your Own Best Friend

Would you talk to your best friend the way you talk to yourself? Probably not. So be kind to yourself and talk to yourself in a way that you would talk to a friend.

Find a Mentor or Coach

If you are struggling to practise positive self-talk on your own, you might consider finding a mentor or coach who can help you. A mentor or coach can provide you with support and guidance, and they can help you develop the skills you need to practise positive self-talk.

Practice Makes Perfect

Positive self-talk, a skill worthy of cultivation, demands time and dedication. Just as a skilled artist refines their craft, your inner dialogue gains depth and harmony through consistent practice. As you tend to the garden of self-encouragement, your mood and confidence blossom, akin to a caterpillar becoming a splendid butterfly. Resist surrender; let dedication be your guide through doubt's tempest. Amid challenges, your commitment to positive self-talk lights the way to aspirations. With each affirmation, you sculpt a destiny, shedding self-limiting beliefs and revealing your masterpiece within. So, persist in practice. This alchemy transforms thoughts into achievements.

LIFE TRANSFORMATIONS: GRATITUDE AND SELF-TALK STORIES

"The more grateful you are, the happier you will be."

– Zig Ziglar

Jillian Michaels

Jillian has been open about her struggles with weight loss and body image. She has said that she was bullied as a child because of her weight, and that she developed an eating disorder as a way to cope with her feelings of insecurity. In her early twenties, she decided to make a change and started working out regularly. She also began to focus on positive self-talk, and she eventually lost over 100 pounds. Today, Jillian Michaels is a successful fitness guru and author. She helps others to achieve their fitness goals through her books, videos, and TV shows. She is also an advocate for body positivity and acceptance.

Jon Kralik

Jon Kralik is a writer who was diagnosed with cancer at the age of 35. He wrote a book about his experience called The Happiness of Forgetting, in which he discusses how gratitude and positive self-talk helped him to cope with his illness. In his book, Kralik writes about how he used gratitude to find meaning in his experience with cancer. He also writes about how positive self-talk helped him to stay motivated and hopeful during his treatment. Kralik's story is an inspiration to anyone who is facing a challenge in their life.

Brené Brown is a research professor who studies shame, vulnerability, and courage. She has found that gratitude can help people to overcome shame and vulnerability. She has written several books on the topic, including Daring Greatly and Rising Strong. In her books, Brown writes about how gratitude can help us connect with others and to build stronger relationships. She also writes about how gratitude can help us be more authentic and to live a more fulfilling life.

These are just a few examples of the many people who have transformed their lives through gratitude and positive self-talk. If you are struggling with challenges in your life, I encourage you to try these techniques. They will help you turn your life around.

> *"Positive self-talk is the process of talking to yourself in a way that is encouraging and supportive."*
>
> *— Amy Morin*

Deepak Chopra

Deepak Chopra, a renowned author, speaker, and spiritual teacher, is an inspiring example of an individual who has transformed his life through the practices of gratitude and positive self-talk. He emphasises the power of these practices in cultivating a positive mindset, enhancing well-being, and attracting abundance into one's life.

Deepak Chopra's personal story is a testament to his own journey to self-transformation. Through his teachings and writings, he encourages individuals to shift their focus from negativity and self-doubt to gratitude and self-affirmation. He advocates for the daily practice of gratitude, where individuals consciously acknowledge and appreciate the blessings in their lives, no matter how small.

Additionally, Deepak Chopra emphasises the importance of positive self-talk as a tool for self-empowerment and personal growth. He encourages individuals to replace negative self-talk with affirmations and positive statements that reinforce self-belief and potential. By rewiring negative thought patterns and replacing them with positive and empowering narratives, individuals can create a more optimistic and fulfilling life.

Deepak Chopra's teachings and personal experiences serve as an inspiration for countless individuals who have embarked on their own transformative journeys. His insights and guidance on gratitude and positive self-talk have helped individuals overcome challenges, find inner peace, and manifest their dreams.

"Every time you are tempted to react in the same old way, ask if you want to be a prisoner of the past or a pioneer of the future."

— Deepak Chopra

Through this powerful quote, he reminds us that we have the power to break free from old patterns and limitations, and instead, embrace a future of endless possibilities. By choosing gratitude and positive self-talk, we can reshape our destinies and create a life filled with purpose and joy. Deepak Chopra's wisdom continues to resonate, guiding countless souls towards self-discovery and the realization of their true potential. His impact as an inspirational figure and transformative teacher will undoubtedly endure for generations to come.

6
THE POWER OF FORGIVENESS

"If you cannot forgive, you will be imprisoned by your own anger and resentment."

— Thich Nhat Hanh

Forgiveness is a profound and transformative act that has the power to increase positive energy in our lives. Forgiveness is a conscious, deliberate decision to release feelings of resentment or vengeance toward a person or group who has harmed you, regardless of whether they actually deserve your forgiveness or not. When we choose to forgive, we make a conscious choice to let go of negative emotions and find inner peace. It's important to note that forgiveness does not mean condoning or forgetting the actions that caused us pain. Rather, it is about releasing the emotional burden that resentment and anger create within us. As Melody Beattie, author and advocate for personal growth, once said, "Forgiveness is unlocking the door to set someone free and realising you were the prisoner!" Forgiveness creates a space for healing and positive energy to flow into our lives. When we hold on to grudges and resentment, we allow negative emotions to control us and drain our energy. But forgiveness liberates us from these emotional burdens, allowing us to experience greater joy, peace, and emotional well-being. Forgiveness has the power to transform our relationships, both with others and ourselves. It enables us to let go of the past, heal wounds, and cultivate empathy and understanding. As Brené Brown, a renowned researcher and author, wisely said, *"Forgiveness is not about forgetting. It is about letting go of another person's throat."*

By forgiving, we release the grip that negative experiences have on us and open ourselves up to new possibilities for connection and growth. When we hold on to grudges and refuse to forgive, we remain stuck in a cycle of negativity and bitterness. This not only affects our mental and emotional well-being but also spills over into other areas of our lives, such as our physical health and relationships. Research by psychologist Robert

Emmons suggests that forgiveness is associated with many benefits, including reduced stress, improved immune function, and enhanced psychological well-being (Emmons, 2007). By choosing forgiveness, we free ourselves from the heavy weight of anger and resentment, and we create space for love, compassion, and joy to flourish. Forgiveness is a gift we give ourselves, as it allows us to move forward and live a more authentic and fulfilling life. As Anne Lamott beautifully expressed, "Not forgiving is like drinking rat poison and then waiting for the rat to die." It's time to release the poison and embrace the transformative power of forgiveness.

In the next section of this chapter, we will explore the benefits of forgiveness, delving into how it can bring us increased peace and improved relationships. Through real-life examples and research, we will see the profound impact forgiveness can have on our well-being. So, let's continue on this journey of understanding and healing, knowing that forgiveness is a powerful tool for cultivating positive energy in our lives.

THE BENEFITS OF FORGIVENESS

Forgiveness is not only a powerful act of letting go and finding inner peace, but it also brings a myriad of benefits to our lives. When we choose to forgive, we open ourselves up to a world of possibilities and experiences that can greatly enhance our well-being and relationships.

Peacefulness

One of the significant benefits of forgiveness is the profound sense of peace it can bring. By releasing the grip of anger, resentment, and bitterness, we free ourselves from the emotional burden that weighs us down. Research by Martin Seligman, a pioneer in positive psychology, suggests that forgiveness is strongly linked to increased happiness and life satisfaction (Seligman, 2006). When we let go of negativity, we create space for positivity and peace to flourish within us.

Improved Relationships

Forgiveness also has the power to improve our relationships. Holding onto grudges and harbouring resentment can create walls of separation and hinder connection with others.

However, when we choose forgiveness, we open the door to reconciliation and healing. By extending forgiveness to others, we demonstrate empathy, compassion, and a willingness to understand their perspectives. Many times, not unforgiveness shortens the life of our good relationships, we tend to lose good people around. With forgiveness, we will be able to keep those good relationships in our lives.

Freedom from Victimhood

Forgiveness allows us to break free from the cycle of blame and victimhood, enabling us to rebuild trust and strengthen relationships. It fosters a climate of understanding and promotes healthier communication patterns. As Stephen Schueller and Acacia C. Parks, psychologists specialising in positive psychology interventions explain, "Forgiveness can facilitate the repair of damaged relationships and create a foundation for trust, openness, and intimacy" (Schueller & Parks, 2014).

Moreover, forgiveness has a positive impact on our mental and emotional well-being. Letting go of negative emotions associated with past hurts reduces stress, anxiety, and depression. We will be able to channel our energy into more productive and positive things. Research by psychologist

Emily Esfahani Smith suggests that forgiveness is associated with increased resilience, positive emotions, and overall psychological well-being (Smith, 2017). When we forgive, we experience a sense of liberation and empowerment. We regain control over our lives and emotions, rather than allowing the actions of others to define us. By choosing forgiveness, we reclaim our personal power and focus our energy on growth, healing, and self-improvement. It enables us to move forward and create a brighter future for ourselves.

Forgiveness also has a ripple effect that extends beyond ourselves. As we cultivate forgiveness within, we become more understanding and compassionate individuals, capable of extending forgiveness to others. By modelling forgiveness in our relationships, we inspire a culture of understanding, empathy, and growth.

FORGIVENESS SETS US FREE

Consider the story of Nelson Mandela, who forgave his captors and worked towards reconciliation and unity in South Africa. Mandela's forgiveness not only brought peace to his own heart, but also inspired a nation and transformed the course of history. His words, "As I walked out the door toward the gate that would lead to my freedom, I knew if I didn't leave my bitterness and hatred behind, I'd still be in prison", reflect the profound impact of forgiveness on his personal and collective journey.

In the next section, we will explore practical techniques for practicing forgiveness, including letting go of grudges and cultivating empathy. Through these techniques, we can actively engage in the process of forgiveness and experience its transformative effects first hand. So, let us embark on this journey of healing and growth, knowing that forgiveness has the power to increase peace within ourselves and foster improved relationships with others.

THE ROLE OF SELF-FORGIVENESS

Self-forgiveness plays a crucial role in our personal healing and growth journey. Understand and accept your shortcomings. By embracing self-forgiveness, we create space for healing emotional wounds, nurturing our well-being, and rebuilding our sense of self.

One of the key aspects of self-forgiveness is understanding the essence behind it. It is about acknowledging our humanness and accepting that we are not perfect. We all make mistakes, and self-forgiveness allows us to let go of the self-judgment and guilt associated with those mistakes. It is a conscious decision to free ourselves from the grip of negative emotions that can hold us back from moving forward.

Self-forgiveness is closely tied to our emotional well-being. When we hold on to self-blame, guilt, and shame, it can take a toll on our mental and emotional health. These negative emotions can lead to self-destructive behaviours, low self-esteem, and a negative self-image. By forgiving ourselves, we release these burdens, creating space for healing, inner peace, and a positive self-image to flourish.

Furthermore, self-forgiveness acts as a catalyst for personal growth. It requires us to take responsibility for our actions and learn from our mistakes. When we forgive ourselves, we acknowledge our capacity to grow, evolve, and change. It opens the doors to self-improvement and the development of resilience and self-compassion. Self-forgiveness is an opportunity to cultivate a mindset that embraces mistakes as valuable lessons rather than permanent failures.

Self-forgiveness and self-compassion go hand in hand. When we extend compassion and kindness to ourselves, we create a nurturing and supportive relationship with our own selves. Self-compassion enables us to hold space for our vulnerabilities, acknowledging that we are deserving of forgiveness and understanding. By cultivating self-compassion, we create a foundation that supports the process of self-forgiveness.

Breaking the cycle of self-judgment and guilt is another significant aspect of self-forgiveness. Often, we can become trapped in negative patterns of self-condemnation, replaying past mistakes over and over again. Self-forgiveness breaks this cycle by allowing us to let go of self-condemnation and embrace forgiveness. It frees us from the weight of the past, liberating us to focus on personal growth and self-acceptance.

Empowerment is an inherent aspect of self-forgiveness. When we forgive ourselves, we reclaim our power, autonomy, and self-worth. We recognise that we have the ability to let go of the past, make amends, and create a brighter future for ourselves. Self-forgiveness is an empowering act that enables us to take charge of our lives and shape our own narratives.

Moreover, self-forgiveness contributes to building resilience. It allows us to navigate through life's challenges and setbacks with a mindset that embraces mistakes as valuable learning experiences. When we forgive ourselves, we cultivate the resilience to bounce back, adapt, and grow stronger from adversity. Self-forgiveness acts as a protective shield against self-sabotaging beliefs and allows us to embrace our potential for growth.

In conclusion, the role of self-forgiveness is vital in our journey towards personal healing and growth. By extending compassion, understanding, and acceptance of ourselves, we create a nurturing environment for healing emotional wounds and rebuilding our sense of self. Self-forgiveness liberates us from the grip of self-judgment and guilt, empowering us to embrace personal growth, cultivate resilience, and live a more fulfilling life.

TECHNIQUES FOR PRACTICING FORGIVENESS: LETTING GO OF GRUDGES & CULTIVATING EMPATHY

"Forgiveness is not an occasional act; it is a permanent attitude."

— Desmond Tutu

Practicing forgiveness is a transformative journey that requires intentional effort and a commitment to personal growth. While forgiveness may seem challenging, there are practical techniques and strategies we can employ to facilitate the process and experience its profound effects. In this section, we will explore two key techniques: Letting go of grudges and cultivating empathy.

Letting Go of Grudges

Letting go of grudges is an essential step in the forgiveness process. It involves releasing the negative emotions associated with past hurts and choosing to move forward with a compassionate and open heart. Here are practical steps to help you let go of grudges:

- **Acknowledge the Pain:** Start by acknowledging the pain and hurt caused by the person or situation. Allow yourself to experience and validate your emotions without judgment.

- **Understand the Perspective:** Try to understand the other person's perspective and motivations. This doesn't mean condoning their actions, but gaining insight into their circumstances and recognising their humanity.

- **Practice Self-Compassion:** Extend compassion towards yourself for the pain you've experienced. Treat yourself with kindness and understanding, recognising that forgiveness is a process that takes time and self-care.

- **Challenge Negative Thoughts:** Identify and challenge negative thoughts and beliefs related to the situation. Replace them with more compassionate and empowering thoughts. For example, instead of dwelling on thoughts of revenge, focus on thoughts of growth and healing.

- **Release Resentment through Forgiveness Rituals:** Engage in forgiveness rituals that resonate with you, such as writing a forgiveness letter, creating a symbolic act of release, or engaging in mindfulness practices to let go of negative emotions.

Cultivating Empathy

Cultivating empathy is another vital aspect of the forgiveness process. Empathy allows us to understand and connect with the experiences and emotions of others, promoting a deeper sense of compassion and forgiveness. Here are practical techniques to cultivate empathy:

- **Active Listening:** Practice active listening when engaging with others. Truly listen to their stories, emotions, and perspectives without judgment or interruption. Seek to understand their experiences and validate their feelings.

- **Put Yourself in Others' Shoes:** Imagine yourself in the other person's position. Consider the factors that may have influenced their actions and the emotions they might have felt. This helps foster understanding and empathy.

- **Seek Common Ground:** Look for commonalities and shared experiences with the person you're forgiving. Focus on the qualities that connect you rather than the differences. Recognise that we are all imperfect and capable of making mistakes.

- **Practice Compassionate Communication:** Communicate with kindness, empathy, and respect. Use "I" statements to express your feelings and needs without blaming or criticising the other person. Encourage open and honest dialogue that promotes understanding and healing.

Practice Self-Reflection and Self-Forgiveness

Self-reflection is an essential aspect of forgiveness that involves examining our own actions, attitudes, and behaviours. It requires us to take responsibility for our part in a situation and acknowledge any harm we may have caused. Here are practical steps to practise self-reflection and self-forgiveness:

- **Acknowledge and Accept Responsibility:** Reflect on your actions and behaviour that contributed to the situation. Take ownership of any mistakes or harm caused and accept responsibility for your part in it.

- **Learn from the Experience:** Identify lessons or insights you can gain from the situation. Reflect on how you can grow and improve as a person based on what you've learned.

- **Practice Self-Compassion and Self-Forgiveness:** Treat yourself with kindness and compassion. Recognise that we are all imperfect and make mistakes. Forgive yourself for any past actions or behaviours that may have caused harm.

- **Take Positive Action:** Once you have acknowledged your part and forgiven yourself, commit to making positive changes moving forward. Take actions that align with your values and contribute to personal growth and healing.

Engage in Therapeutic Support

Seeking professional therapeutic support can be incredibly beneficial in the forgiveness process, particularly in situations involving deep emotional wounds or trauma. Therapists and counsellors can provide a safe and supportive space for exploring emotions, gaining insights, and developing strategies for forgiveness. Here's how therapeutic support can assist in forgiveness:

- **Emotional Processing:** Therapists can guide individuals in processing and expressing their emotions related to the forgiveness journey. They provide tools and techniques to help navigate complex emotions and facilitate healing.

- **Perspective Shifting:** Therapists can help individuals gain a new perspective on the situation and the person they are forgiving. They can challenge negative beliefs and assist in reframing the narrative, allowing for a more compassionate understanding.

- **Healing Trauma:** In cases where forgiveness involves healing from deep emotional wounds or trauma, therapists can provide specialised interventions and techniques to address and heal these wounds effectively.

- **Developing Forgiveness Strategies:** Therapists can assist individuals in developing personalised forgiveness strategies based on their unique needs and circumstances. They offer guidance, support, and practical techniques to facilitate the forgiveness process.

Embrace Gratitude and Compassion

Gratitude and compassion are powerful antidotes to resentment and anger, and they can support the forgiveness journey. By cultivating gratitude and compassion, we open our hearts and minds to the transformative power of forgiveness. Here's how to embrace gratitude and compassion in the forgiveness process:

- **Gratitude Practice:** Incorporate a regular gratitude practice into your daily life. Take time each day to reflect on things you are grateful for, including the lessons learned from challenging experiences.

- **Acts of Kindness:** Engage in acts of kindness towards others. Practice compassion and empathy by extending understanding and forgiveness to those around you. Minor acts of kindness can have a ripple effect and foster forgiveness in both parties involved.

- **Loving-Kindness Meditation:** Practice loving-kindness meditation, where you extend well-wishes and loving thoughts towards yourself and others, including the person you are forgiving. This meditation cultivates compassion and fosters forgiveness.

- **Cultivate Empathy:** Continuously work on cultivating empathy towards others, recognising their humanity, and understanding their perspectives and experiences. This helps develop a compassionate and forgiving mindset.

Write a Letter of Forgiveness

Writing a letter of forgiveness is a powerful and cathartic exercise that allows you to express your feelings, thoughts, and forgiveness to the person who has hurt you. While you may or may not choose to send the letter, the act of writing it can be incredibly healing. Here's how to write a letter of forgiveness:

- **Find a Quiet and Comfortable Space:** Choose a peaceful environment where you can focus and reflect without distractions. Create a calming atmosphere by lighting a candle or playing soft music if it helps you relax.

- **Address the Person Directly:** Begin the letter by addressing the person you are forgiving. Use their name or any other appropriate form of address.

- **Express Your Feelings:** Start by expressing your emotions honestly and openly. Share how their actions or words affected you and acknowledge the pain you experienced.

- **Practice Empathy:** Try to understand the other person's perspective and the reasons behind their actions. This doesn't justify their behaviour but helps you develop compassion and empathy.

- **Declare Your Forgiveness:** Clearly state that you forgive the person for what they have done. Use words that convey your intention to release the anger, resentment, and hurt associated with the situation.

- **Reflect on Personal Growth:** Share any insights or lessons you have gained from the experience. Acknowledge how it has shaped you as a person and helped you grow stronger.

- **Express Gratitude (optional):** If you feel comfortable, you can express gratitude for the lessons learned or any positive aspects that emerged from the situation. However, this step is optional and depends on your personal circumstances.

- **Closure and Release:** Conclude the letter with a sense of closure and release. State that you are letting go of any negative emotions and moving forward with love, peace, and freedom.

- **Decide whether to Send or Keep the Letter:** Consider whether you want to send the letter or keep it for yourself as a symbolic act of forgiveness. The decision is entirely up to you, and both options can be equally powerful.

Writing a letter of forgiveness provides a space for emotional release, self-reflection, and the opportunity to let go of negative emotions. It allows you to find closure within yourself, even if the other person is unaware of the letter. Remember, the act of forgiveness is primarily for your own healing and growth.

Each technique discussed here offers a unique approach to forgiving others and ourselves, promoting positive energy and emotional well-being. Adding these techniques into your forgiveness journey, you can navigate the path towards peace, healing, and personal transformation.

HEALING THROUGH FORGIVENESS: PERSONAL STORIES OF FREEDOM

It is wise for us to learn from the stories and experiences of others. Many times, it helps us to know what to do. In some other instances, it provides encouragement and courage, and inspiration for us to positively handle ours. Here are a few stories to learn from.

Thich Nhat Hanh

Thich Nhat Hanh was a Vietnamese Buddhist monk, peace activist, and author. He was a leading figure in the anti-war movement in Vietnam and a proponent of nonviolence. He taught that forgiveness is essential for peace, saying, "If you cannot forgive, you will be imprisoned by your own anger and resentment." Thich Nhat Hanh learned the power of forgiveness from his own experience. He was imprisoned in a Vietnamese prison for 10 years for his opposition to the war. During his time in prison, he learned to forgive his captors and to see them as victims of the war as well. Thich Nhat Hanh's teachings on forgiveness have inspired people all over the world. He is a powerful example of how forgiveness can be used to overcome hatred and violence.

Desmond Tutu

Desmond Tutu was a South African Anglican archbishop and anti-apartheid activist. He was awarded the Nobel Peace Prize in 1984 for his nonviolent opposition to apartheid. He was a strong advocate for forgiveness, saying, *"Forgiveness is not an occasional act; it is a permanent attitude."* Tutu learned the power of forgiveness from his own experience. He witnessed the horrors of apartheid first hand, but he never gave up hope for a peaceful resolution. He believed that forgiveness was the only way to break the cycle of violence and hatred. Tutu's teachings on forgiveness have inspired people all over the world. He is a powerful example of how forgiveness can be used to overcome oppression and injustice.

These stories teach us to not hold on to past hurts as they have all the potentials to weigh our lives down in every sense. Letting go of grudges and forgiving those who have wronged us will help us live a victorious life. When we hold on to grudges, we are going to spread negativity to other people.

Eva Kor

Eva Kor was a Holocaust survivor and an advocate for forgiveness and peace. She, along with her twin sister Miriam, endured unimaginable horrors at the Auschwitz concentration camp during World War II.

Despite the immense suffering she experienced, Eva Kor chose to forgive her captors and the Nazi regime. She believed that forgiveness was a way to free herself from the burden of hatred and anger. Eva dedicated her life to sharing her story and promoting forgiveness and healing. She founded the CANDLES Holocaust Museum and Education Centre, where she taught the power of forgiveness to thousands of people.

Eva's personal journey of forgiveness and her message of healing resonated with people around the world. She touched the lives of many, emphasising the importance of forgiveness as a transformative and empowering act. Eva Kor's remarkable story serves as a testament to the strength of the human spirit and the potential for healing and freedom that forgiveness can bring, even in the face of unimaginable atrocities.

7
OVERCOMING FEAR & ANXIETY

"The brave man is not he who does not feel afraid, but he who conquers that fear"

– Nelson Mandela

Fear and anxiety are powerful emotions that have the potential to hold us back from living a positive and fulfilling life. Understanding the nature of fear and anxiety is crucial in order to effectively overcome their grip and create a life filled with positivity and growth. Fear can be defined as an emotional response to a perceived threat or danger. It is a natural and instinctual reaction that evolved as a means of self-preservation. It is an innate response to perceived threats that originate in the amygdala, a small almond-shaped structure in the brain. As Fredrickson (2009) explains, the amygdala is responsible for processing emotions and detecting potential dangers. When confronted with a fear-inducing stimulus, the amygdala triggers a cascade of physiological responses, releasing stress hormones such as adrenaline, which leads to heightened arousal and increased vigilance. Simultaneously, the prefrontal cortex, as described by Kahneman (2011), may temporarily become inhibited, reducing our ability to engage in rational decision-making and emotional regulation. When we encounter a real or imagined threat, our bodies trigger a fight-or-flight response, preparing us to either confront or escape the danger. However, fear can also manifest in response to situations that are not inherently life-threatening, such as public speaking, making important decisions, or trying something new. While fear is often an immediate response to tangible threats, anxiety arises from uncertain or future-oriented worries.

Seligman (2011) notes that anxiety can stem from an overactive amygdala and a compromised prefrontal cortex, resulting in chronic apprehension. This persistent anxiety cycle inhibits our ability to function optimally and may lead to symptoms such as excessive worry, restlessness, and an inability to relax. Anxiety, on the other hand, is a more pervasive and generalised state of fear. It often arises from a sense of uncertainty and anticipation of future events or outcomes. Anxiety can be characterised by excessive worry, restlessness, difficulty concentrating, and physical symptoms like rapid heartbeat and shortness of breath. Unlike fear, which is typically triggered by an immediate threat, anxiety can persist over time and interfere with our daily lives.

Fear and anxiety can have significant negative effects on our personal lives. Dweck (2006) emphasises that fear of failure can hinder personal growth and limit individuals from pursuing new opportunities or taking risks necessary for self-improvement. This fear-induced avoidance behaviour prevents us from fully engaging in activities that bring joy and fulfilment, undermining our overall well-being. Additionally, fear and anxiety can erode self-esteem and confidence, as noted by Bryant (2019), fostering self-doubt and inhibiting our ability to achieve our full potential. Fear and anxiety also affect our social interactions and relationships. Keltner (2016) explains that social anxiety, driven by the fear of judgment or rejection, can cause individuals to withdraw from social situations and isolate themselves. This avoidance behaviour impairs the formation of meaningful connections and can lead to a sense of loneliness and isolation. Furthermore, fear-based insecurities can strain relationships, hindering open communication and fostering mistrust, as observed by Rogers (1961).

Both fear and anxiety can significantly impact our overall well-being and limit our potential for personal growth. They can prevent us from taking risks, pursuing new opportunities, and fully embracing positive experiences. When fear and anxiety hold us back, we miss out on valuable opportunities for self-discovery, development, and connection with others. To live a positive life, it is essential to confront and overcome our fears and anxieties. This requires a willingness to understand and challenge the thoughts and beliefs that fuel our fears. Often, our fears are rooted in negative assumptions and catastrophic thinking, magnifying the potential risks and downplaying our abilities to cope and adapt.

IDENTIFYING FEAR AND ANXIETY

"Nothing in life is to be feared. It is only to be to understood"

– Marie Curie

In order to overcome fear and anxiety, it is important to first recognise and identify them in our lives. Sometimes, fear and anxiety can manifest in subtle ways, making it necessary to develop self-awareness and keen observation. By understanding the nature of our fears and anxieties, we can effectively address them and take steps towards a more positive and fulfilling life.

Self-Reflection

Take some time for self-reflection and introspection. Ask yourself what situations, thoughts, or experiences trigger fear or anxiety within you. Be honest and open with yourself. This is an important step in recognising and understanding your fears.

Emotional and Physical Responses

Pay attention to your emotional and physical responses in various situations. Fear and anxiety can manifest differently in different individuals. Notice any patterns of increased heart rate, tense muscles, racing thoughts, or feelings of unease. These signs can serve as indicators of underlying fears and anxieties.

Thought Patterns

Observe your thought patterns and the narratives you tell yourself. Are there recurring negative thoughts or self-limiting beliefs that contribute to your fears and anxieties? Notice the specific thoughts that arise when you encounter challenging or unfamiliar situations. If you push against those thought patterns, you will see yourself doing marvellous things. As Henry Ford said, *"One of the greatest discoveries a man makes, one of his great surprises, is to find he can do what he was afraid he couldn't do."*

Triggers

Identify the specific triggers that evoke fear or anxiety within you. It could be public speaking, social interactions, uncertainty about the future, or past traumatic experiences. Understanding your triggers can help you anticipate and prepare for situations that may provoke these emotions.

Impact on Daily Life

Reflect on how fear and anxiety impact your daily life. Do they hinder you from pursuing your goals, engaging in meaningful relationships, or trying new experiences? Recognise the ways in which fear and anxiety may be holding you back from living a positive and fulfilling life.

Journaling

Keep a journal to document your fears and anxieties. Write down your thoughts and emotions surrounding specific situations or triggers. This practice can help you gain clarity and insight into the underlying causes of your fears, as well as track your progress in overcoming them.

Seek Feedback

Trusted friends, family members, or professionals can provide valuable insights into your fears and anxieties. Engage in open conversations with them, sharing your experiences and seeking their perspective. Sometimes, an outside perspective can shed light on aspects of your fears that you may not have considered.

Remember, identifying fear and anxiety is the first step towards overcoming them. By being attentive to your emotions, thoughts, and responses, you can develop a deeper understanding of how fear and anxiety manifest in your life. This self-awareness lays the foundation for developing effective strategies to address and overcome these challenges.

TECHNIQUES FOR OVERCOMING FEAR AND ANXIETY

"He who is not every day conquering fear has not learned the secret of life"

– Ralph Waldo Emerson

Fear and anxiety can be overwhelming and paralysing, but they don't have to control our lives. There are practical techniques and strategies that can help us overcome these challenges and regain a sense of calm and empowerment. By facing our fears and incorporating relaxation techniques into our daily routine, we can gradually reduce the grip of fear and anxiety and live a more fulfilling and positive life.

Face Your Fears

One effective technique for overcoming fear and anxiety is to face them head-on. Start by identifying a fear or anxiety that you want to address. Break it down into smaller, manageable steps and gradually expose yourself to those situations or triggers. As you face your fears in a controlled manner, you build confidence and realise that you can handle challenging situations.

For example, if you have a fear of public speaking, start by speaking in front of a small and supportive group. Gradually increase the audience size and complexity of the speaking engagements. Each step forward will help desensitise you to the fear and build resilience.

Cognitive Restructuring

Our thoughts play a significant role in perpetuating fear and anxiety. Cognitive restructuring involves identifying and challenging negative thought patterns and replacing them with more realistic and positive ones. When you notice yourself engaging in catastrophic thinking or assuming the worst-case scenario, consciously challenge those thoughts by questioning their validity.

For instance, if you're anxious about an upcoming job interview and constantly think, "I'll definitely mess it up," reframe that thought to a more balanced perspective, such as, "I have prepared well, and I will do my best." By consciously changing your thoughts, you can reduce anxiety and approach situations with a more positive mindset.

Relaxation Techniques

Incorporating relaxation techniques into your daily routine can help calm your mind and body, reducing the impact of fear and anxiety. Practices such as deep breathing, progressive muscle relaxation, meditation, and mindfulness can promote a sense of relaxation and inner peace. Deep breathing exercises involve taking slow, deep breaths, inhaling through your nose and exhaling through your mouth. This technique helps activate the body's relaxation response and reduces stress. Progressive muscle relaxation involves tensing and releasing different muscle groups, promoting physical and mental relaxation.

Meditation and mindfulness practices can also train your mind to focus on the present moment and cultivate a non-judgmental awareness of your thoughts and emotions. These practices can help you detach from anxious thoughts and create a sense of inner calm.

Self-Care

Taking care of yourself is crucial in managing fear and anxiety. Engage in activities that bring you joy and relaxation, such as exercising, spending time in nature, pursuing hobbies, or connecting with loved ones. Prioritise sleep, maintain a balanced diet, and limit the consumption of substances like caffeine and alcohol, which can exacerbate anxiety symptoms. By practicing self-care, you create a foundation of well-being that supports your emotional resilience and ability to cope with fear and anxiety.

Seek Professional Support

If fear and anxiety significantly impact your daily life and functioning, it may be beneficial to seek professional support. Therapists, counsellors, or psychologists can provide specialised techniques, guidance, and support tailored to your specific needs. They can help you explore the root causes of your fears and anxieties and develop effective strategies for overcoming them. Recognising the negative impacts of fear and anxiety is crucial for developing effective strategies to overcome them. May (1977) suggests that seeking support from mental health professionals can provide valuable guidance and techniques for managing fear and anxiety. Cognitive-behavioural therapies, as researched by Gregg and Sedikides (2010), can assist individuals in reframing negative thought patterns, challenging irrational beliefs, and developing healthy coping strategies.

Visualisation and Positive Imagery

Visualisation is a powerful technique that involves creating vivid mental images of yourself successfully overcoming a fear or anxiety-inducing situation. Close your eyes and imagine yourself confidently navigating through the situation, feeling calm, and achieving a positive outcome. Engage all your senses to make the visualisation as realistic as possible. By repeatedly visualising success, you can rewire your brain and build confidence in your ability to handle challenging situations.

Supportive Social Connections

Surrounding yourself with a supportive network of family, friends, or support groups can significantly aid in overcoming fear and anxiety. Share your fears and anxieties with trusted individuals who can offer encouragement, guidance, and a listening ear. Engaging in meaningful conversations and connecting with others who have faced similar challenges can provide a sense of validation, perspective, and emotional support. Remember, you don't have to face fear and anxiety alone.

Exposure Therapy

Exposure therapy is a structured approach to gradually confronting and desensitising yourself to specific fears or phobias. Under the guidance of a trained therapist, you systematically expose yourself to the fear-inducing stimuli in a safe and controlled manner. By repeatedly exposing yourself to the fear trigger while practicing relaxation techniques and utilising coping strategies, you can reduce the intensity of your fear response over time. Exposure therapy is highly effective in treating various anxiety disorders and specific phobias.

As we delve into techniques for overcoming fear and anxiety, let's explore personal stories of individuals who have successfully conquered their fears and found freedom on the other side. Their experiences will inspire and demonstrate the power of resilience and determination in the face of fear and anxiety. Think on this quote from Marilyn Monroe "We should all start to live before we get too old. Fear is stupid. So are regrets".

BUILDING RESILIENCE: STRATEGIES FOR NURTURING MENTAL STRENGTH

Resilience is a powerful trait that enables individuals to adapt, bounce back, and thrive in the face of adversity. It is a key factor in maintaining mental well-being and achieving personal growth. Building resilience requires intentional efforts to nurture mental strength and develop effective strategies to cope with life's challenges. By incorporating various techniques into daily life, individuals can cultivate resilience and enhance their ability to navigate through difficult times.

Developing a Growth Mindset:

- Embrace challenges as opportunities for growth and learning.

- View setbacks as temporary and see them as stepping stones towards success.

- Foster a belief in personal potential and the ability to overcome obstacles.

- Cultivate a positive outlook and maintain optimism even in difficult circumstances.

Cultivating Emotional Intelligence:

- Enhance self-awareness to understand and manage emotions effectively.
- Develop empathy and the ability to understand and connect with others' emotions.
- Practice emotional regulation to navigate through challenging situations.
- Cultivate strong interpersonal skills and build positive relationships.

Building Social Support:

- Surround yourself with a supportive network of friends, family, and mentors.
- Seek guidance and encouragement from individuals who uplift and inspire you.
- Share struggles and challenges with trusted individuals to gain perspective and support.

- Engage in meaningful connections and contribute to the well-being of others.

Practicing Self-Care:

- Prioritise physical, emotional, and mental well-being.
- Engage in regular exercise to reduce stress and promote overall health.
- Get sufficient sleep to rejuvenate and recharge the mind and body.
- Engage in activities that bring joy, relaxation, and fulfilment.

Cultivating Problem-Solving Skills:

- Develop effective problem-solving techniques to approach challenges.
- Break down problems into smaller, manageable steps.
- Seek creative solutions and think outside the box.

- Learn from experiences and apply knowledge to future situations.

Maintaining a Positive Mindset:

- Challenge negative thoughts and reframe them with positive perspectives.

- Practice gratitude and focus on the things you appreciate in life.

- Surround yourself with positive influences and inspirational content.

- Celebrate insignificant victories and acknowledge the progress made.

Incorporating these strategies into daily life can empower individuals to build resilience and nurture their mental strength. By developing a growth mindset, cultivating emotional intelligence, building a supportive network, practicing self-care, cultivating problem-solving skills, and maintaining a positive mindset, individuals can enhance their ability to bounce back from adversity, overcome challenges, and thrive in all aspects of life. Building resilience is a lifelong journey that requires commitment and practice, but the rewards are immense in terms of personal growth, well-being, and achieving success.

CONQUERING FEAR: INSPIRING STORIES OF DREAM ACHIEVEMENT

Michael Jordan

Michael Jordan was a basketball player who is widely considered being one of the greatest of all time. He won six NBA championships with the Chicago Bulls, and he was a five-time NBA MVP. But Jordan's journey to success was not without its challenges. Jordan was a shy child who was afraid of public speaking. He also had a fear of failure. But Jordan overcame these fears through hard work and determination. He practiced for hours every day, and he never gave up on his dreams.

One of the most famous examples of Jordan's fear of public speaking came during his rookie year in the NBA. He was scheduled to give a speech at a team event, but he was so nervous that he couldn't even get the words out. He ended up running off the stage in tears. After that experience, Jordan vowed to overcome his fear of public speaking. He started by practicing in front of a mirror. Then, he started giving speeches to small groups of people. Eventually, he worked his way up to giving speeches in front of sizeable crowds.

Jordan's story is an inspiration to anyone who has ever struggled with fear or anxiety. It shows that it is possible to overcome these challenges and achieve your goals, no matter how difficult they may seem.

Lady Gaga

Lady Gaga is a singer, songwriter, and actress who has won numerous awards, including six Grammy Awards. Nevertheless, Gaga's journey to success was not without its challenges. Gaga has spoken openly about her struggles with anxiety and depression. She said that she used to have panic attacks so severe that she would have to cancel shows. But Gaga has learned to manage her anxiety and has become one of the most successful pop stars in the world.

One of the most difficult times in Gaga's life came in 2013, when she was diagnosed with post-traumatic stress disorder (PTSD). PTSD is a mental health condition that can develop after a person experiences a traumatic event. In Gaga's case, the traumatic event was a sexual assault that she experienced when she was 19 years old. Gaga's PTSD caused her to have severe anxiety attacks. She would often feel like she was going to die. She also had nightmares and flashbacks about the assault. Gaga sought professional help for her PTSD. She worked with a therapist to learn how to manage her anxiety and cope with the trauma. She also started taking medication to help with her symptoms.

After years of therapy and medication, Gaga is now able to manage her PTSD. She is still working on her recovery, but she is grateful for the progress that she has made. Gaga's story is an inspiration to anyone who has ever struggled with anxiety or PTSD. It shows that it is possible to overcome these challenges and live a happy and fulfilling life.

Emma Stone

Emma Stone is an actress who has won an Academy Award, a Golden Globe Award, and a BAFTA Award, and she is an example of someone who overcame her fears. Stone has spoken openly about her struggles with anxiety. She has said that she used to be so afraid of public speaking that she would have to take medication to calm down. But

Stone has learned to manage her anxiety and has starred in many successful movies. One of the most difficult times in Stone's life came when she was filming the movie "The Amazing Spider-Man". She was so anxious about the role that she had to be hospitalised.

After that experience, Stone sought professional help for her anxiety. She worked with a therapist to learn how to manage her anxiety and cope with the stress of her job. She also started taking medication to help with her symptoms. After years of therapy and medication, Stone is now able to manage her anxiety. She is still working on her recovery, but she is grateful for the progress that she has made. Stone's story is an inspiration to anyone who has ever struggled with anxiety. It shows that it is possible to overcome these challenges and live a happy and fulfilling life.

Keanu Reeves

Keanu Reeves is an actor who has starred in many successful movies, including "The Matrix" and "John Wick". Reeves also spoke openly about his struggles with anxiety and depression. He has said that he used to have panic attacks so severe that he would have to leave the room. But Reeves has learned to manage his anxiety and has gone on to become one of the most successful actors in Hollywood. One of the most difficult times in Reeves' life came when his girlfriend, Jennifer Syme, died in a car accident in 2001. Syme was pregnant with Reeves' child. At the time of her death, Reeves was devastated by Syme's death. He said that he felt "like a part of me died". He struggled with depression and anxiety for many years.

In 2011, Reeves spoke about his struggles for the first time in an interview with Parade magazine. He said that he had "hit rock bottom" and that he was "lost and alone". Reeves said that he eventually found help through therapy and medication. He said that he is now "on the road to recovery".

Reeves' story is an inspiration to anyone who has ever struggled with grief, depression, or anxiety. It shows that it is possible to overcome these challenges and live a happy and fulfilling life.

Serena Williams

As one of the greatest tennis players of all time, Serena's journey to success has been marked by numerous obstacles and challenges that tested her mental and emotional strength. Throughout her career, she has battled injuries, faced criticism, and dealt with the pressures of competition at the highest level. Despite these adversities, Serena has consistently shown unwavering resilience and determination, proving that fear and anxiety can be transformed into powerful catalysts for growth.

Serena's story is one of courage and perseverance. She has never shied away from acknowledging her fears, but has rather embraced them as opportunities to push herself beyond her limits. By embracing her vulnerabilities, Serena has demonstrated that true strength lies in confronting and conquering one's fears. She has used her experiences of fear and anxiety to fuel her passion for the game and motivate herself to continuously improve.

Beyond her remarkable achievements on the tennis court, Serena has become an empowering figure for people around the world. Through her journey, she has shown that success is not defined solely by victories and trophies, but by the inner strength and resilience one possesses. Serena's story resonates with individuals who face their own fears and anxieties, inspiring them to pursue their dreams with unwavering determination.

Serena Williams serves as a shining example of how fear and anxiety can be transformed into stepping stones towards greatness. Her ability to rise above adversity and channel her fears into motivation has not only shaped her career, but has also left a lasting impact on the world. By sharing her personal journey, Serena continues to inspire and empower others to overcome their own fears and anxieties, reminding them that they too can achieve their dreams if they have the courage to confront their inner challenges head-on.

Lessons to Learn from these Individuals

- ❖ Don't let fear hold you back. Fear is a natural emotion, but it shouldn't stop you from pursuing your dreams. Remember, the most difficult thing is the decision to act. Once you take that first step, the rest will be easier.

- ❖ Don't be afraid to ask for help. There are people who care about you and want to help you succeed. Don't be afraid to reach out to them for support.

- ❖ Never give up. No matter how difficult things get, never give up on your dreams. If you keep going, you will eventually achieve your goals.

- ❖ They had a support system. They all had people who believed in them and supported them on their journey. This support was essential to their success.

Overcoming fear and anxiety is a challenge, but it's possible with dedication. Cultivating a life of positivity can help you overcome fear and anxiety. When you focus on the positive aspects of your life, it becomes easier to deal with the challenges that come your way. Here are some tips for cultivating a life of positivity. Remember, you are not alone. There are people who care about you and want to help you succeed. Don't give up on your dreams. With hard work and perseverance, you can achieve anything you set your mind to. Ultimately, overcoming fear and anxiety takes time and effort. Be patient and kind to yourself throughout the process. Celebrate small victories and acknowledge your progress. With perseverance and the right techniques, you can break free from the grip of fear and anxiety and cultivate a life of positivity, growth, and well-being.

FIND OUT THE SOURCE OF YOUR FEARS AND ANXIETIES

Fear and anxiety can be very subtle. Through mindfulness and mediation, you can process your emotions and also find out the sources of fear. Then begin to deal with them actively.

8
THE IMPORTANCE OF CONNECTION

"Alone, we can do so little; together, we can do so much"

Helen Keller

Connection is a fundamental aspect of human existence that significantly influences our well-being and positive energy. As social beings, we have an innate need for social interactions and a sense of belonging (Seligman, 2011; Martin, 2012). Connection encompasses various types and levels that contribute to our overall well-being. Interpersonal connections with close friends, family members, and romantic partners play a crucial role in our lives (Fredrickson, 2009; Seligman, 2011). These relationships provide emotional support, companionship, and a sense of belonging. They offer us a safe space to share our thoughts, feelings, and experiences, fostering a deeper understanding of ourselves and others (Keltner, 2009; Dweck, 2006). Broader connections within communities, organisations, or social networks also hold immense value (Chavis et al., 2008; Skidmore et al., 2014). They provide a sense of belonging to something larger than ourselves and offer opportunities for shared experiences, collective goals, and a shared sense of identity (Arnold et al., 2019; Drennon-Gala, 2015).

Community connections can be formed through involvement in volunteer work, participation in group activities, or engagement in shared interests (Cullen, 2012; McMillan, 1996). The concept of Emotional Contagion, as described by scholars like DW McMillan and Tiffany R. Jimenez, further illustrates the impact of connection on our well-being (Jimenez & Hoffman, 2017). Emotional Contagion refers to the phenomenon of emotions spreading from one person to another. When we interact with others, we can "catch" their emotions, whether positive or negative. This process highlights the profound influence that our social connections can have on our emotional states. Being surrounded by positive, supportive individuals can uplift our spirits, enhance our positive emotions, and contribute to a more optimistic outlook on life (Jimenez & Hoffman, 2017; McMillan, 1996). Moreover, Grant et al., (2009) and Hoffman (2009) emphasise the importance of social connections in promoting well-being and positive energy. Social support, derived from strong connections, has been linked to many benefits, including reduced stress levels, improved mental health, enhanced resilience, and increased overall life satisfaction (Hoffman, 2009; Grant et al., 2009). Engaging in meaningful interactions with others allows us to share joys, sorrows, and everyday experiences, fostering a sense of connection and fulfilment.

The importance of connection and community in cultivating a positive life lies in the support, validation, and understanding they offer. When we feel connected, heard, and valued by others, we experience a sense of well-being and fulfilment. Community provides a network of relationships that provide emotional support during difficult times, reducing feelings of loneliness and isolation (Uchino, 2006). Community connections expose us to diverse perspectives, cultures, and experiences. This exposure promotes empathy, tolerance, and open-mindedness, enriching our lives and broadening our horizons. Interacting with a diverse community fosters personal growth, challenges our assumptions, and allows us to learn from others' wisdom and experiences (Haslam et al., 2008). "No one can live without a relationship. You may withdraw into the mountains, become a monk, a sannyasi, wander off into the desert by yourself, but you are related. You cannot escape from that absolute fact. You cannot exist in isolation". This quote by Jiddu Krishnamurti opens our mind to see the fact that no man is an island. We are all related to some people. If we withdraw ourselves from connection with other people, we are sabotaging ourselves, our minds will not be open. It will make us keep a lot of burden to ourselves, instead of discussing it in order to get help.

DANGERS OF ISOLATION

> *"The worst cruelty that can be inflicted on a human being is isolation."*
>
> *— Sukarno*

Isolation from connection and community can have detrimental effects on our mental, emotional, and even physical well-being. The absence of meaningful social bonds and a sense of belonging can lead to various negative outcomes that hinder our ability to cultivate a positive life. Let's explore the dangers of isolation and its impact on our overall well-being. Many studies have highlighted the negative consequences of social isolation and loneliness. Research by Cacioppo and Hawkley (2009) found that social isolation and loneliness are associated with increased risks of developing mental health issues such as depression, anxiety, and cognitive decline. The lack of social support and interaction deprives individuals of the emotional and psychological resources needed to cope with stress and adversity (Hawkley & Cacioppo, 2010).

Moreover, social isolation has been linked to a higher prevalence of physical health problems. A meta-analysis by Holt-Lunstad, Smith, and Layton (2010) demonstrated that social isolation carries a risk comparable to that of smoking, obesity, and high blood pressure in predicting mortality. The absence of social connections negatively impacts our immune system, cardiovascular health, and overall physiological functioning (Holt-Lunstad, 2018). When we are isolated, our mental health can suffer greatly. The absence of social support and connection leaves us vulnerable to negative thought patterns, self-doubt, and low self-esteem (Qualter et al., 2015). Without a sense of belonging and validation from others, we may fall into a cycle of self-sabotage, negative self-talk, and feelings of worthlessness (Baumeister et al., 2005). Isolation can exacerbate feelings of loneliness, which, in turn, can contribute to a downward spiral of emotional distress (Cacioppo& Patrick, 2008).

Additionally, isolation from connection and community can hinder personal growth and limit opportunities for learning and development. When we withdraw from social interactions, we miss out on valuable perspectives, insights, and support that others can offer. Interacting with others exposes us to different ideas, challenges our beliefs, and broadens our horizons (Klohnen & Mendelsohn, 1998). By isolating ourselves, we deny ourselves the chance to engage in new experiences, acquire new skills, and form meaningful relationships that can enrich our lives (Putnam, 2000).

One poignant quote that encapsulates the dangers of isolation comes from psychologist Abraham Maslow, who said, "The fact is that people are good. Give people affection and security, and they will give affection and be secure in their feelings and their behaviour." This quote reminds us of the reciprocal nature of connection and community.

When we withdraw ourselves from others, we deny ourselves the opportunity to receive and give affection, support, and security. We are inherently social beings, wired for connection, and when we isolate ourselves, we deprive ourselves of the nourishment that social bonds provide.

The dangers of isolation extend beyond our individual well-being and also affect our communities. When individuals become disconnected and isolated, it weakens the social fabric of society. Putnam (2000) has highlighted the decline in social capital and community engagement, resulting in decreased trust, civic participation, and cooperation. Without a sense of connection and community, we lose the collective strength that comes from collaboration and shared values. Recognising the dangers of isolation, it becomes clear that cultivating connection and community is vital for a positive life and lifestyle. Building and nurturing social relationships have many benefits for our well-being. It provides us with emotional support, a sense of belonging, and a network of individuals who can offer guidance, encouragement, and validation. Social connections provide a buffer against stress, enhance resilience, and promote overall mental and physical health (Uchino, 2009).

Being part of a community fosters a sense of purpose and meaning in our lives. Through shared goals and collective endeavours, we find opportunities for personal growth, contribution, and a sense of belonging to something greater than ourselves (Baumeister & Leary, 1995). Community involvement and engagement also allow us to make a positive impact on others' lives, fostering a sense of fulfilment and satisfaction (Post, 2005). In the words of Margaret Mead, an influential cultural anthropologist, *"Never doubt that a small group of thoughtful, committed citizens can change the world; indeed, it's the only thing that ever has."* This quote reminds us of the power of community and collective action. When we come together, we have the capacity to bring about positive change, address societal challenges, and create a more inclusive and compassionate world.

GROW IN A COMMUNITY

It is essential to prioritise connection and community in our lives. This can be achieved by actively seeking social interactions, engaging in shared activities, and fostering meaningful relationships. Joining clubs, organisations, or community groups aligned with our interests allows us to connect with like-minded individuals who share our passions and values. Participating in volunteer work and community service provides opportunities to contribute and make a positive impact on others' lives.

BENEFITS OF CULTIVATING CONNECTION

"I alone cannot change the world, but I can cast a stone across the waters to create many ripples."

– Mother Teresa

Cultivating connection and actual community offers a multitude of benefits that positively impact our lives and contribute to a more fulfilling and meaningful existence. When we actively engage in building and maintaining social relationships, we experience a range of advantages that promote our well-being and overall positive energy. Let's explore some of the key benefits of cultivating connection and community.

Emotional Support and Well-Being

Connection and community provide us with a vital source of emotional support. Having individuals we can rely on during challenging times helps alleviate stress, anxiety, and feelings of loneliness (Cohen & Wills, 1985). By sharing our joys, sorrows, and experiences with others, we create a sense of belonging and enhance our overall emotional well-being (Reis et al., 2010). The support and understanding we receive from our social networks can boost our resilience, improve our mood, and promote positive mental health (Thoits, 2011).

Increased Life Satisfaction

Engaging in meaningful connections and being part of a community has been linked to higher levels of life satisfaction. Research by McMillan and Chavis (1986) suggests that individuals who feel a sense of belonging and connection to their communities experience greater life fulfilment. Being surrounded by people who share common values, interests, and goals contributes to a sense of purpose and fulfilment in our lives (Avey et al., 2008). By participating in community activities and forging genuine connections, we can enhance our overall life satisfaction.

Enhanced Physical Health

Cultivating connection and community has a positive impact on our physical health. Many studies have found that individuals with strong social connections have better cardiovascular health, stronger immune systems, and lower rates of mortality (House et al., 1988; Holt-Lunstad et al., 2010). Engaging in social interactions and participating in community activities can promote healthier behaviours, such as exercise, healthy eating, and regular check-ups (Umberson et al., 2010). The social support and encouragement we receive from our connections also contribute to healthier lifestyle choices and overall well-being.

Sense of Belonging and Identity

Connection and community foster a sense of belonging and identity. Being part of a group or community allows us to form a shared identity and experience a sense of belongingness (Baumeister & Leary, 1995). This sense of belonging contributes to our self-esteem, self-worth, and overall sense of identity (Jetten et al., 2012). By connecting with others who share our interests, values, or cultural background, we find validation and acceptance, which in turn boosts our self-confidence and positive self-image.

Opportunities for Growth and Learning

Connection and community provide opportunities for personal growth and learning. Engaging with diverse individuals exposes us to new ideas, perspectives, and experiences (Klohnen & Mendelsohn, 1998). By participating in community activities, we expand our knowledge, skills, and abilities, fostering personal development and growth. The collective wisdom and support within a community create an environment conducive to learning, allowing us to broaden our horizons and continuously evolve as individuals.

BUILDING MEANINGFUL RELATIONSHIPS: STRATEGIES FOR CONNECTIONS

In today's fast-paced and interconnected world, fostering meaningful connections has become increasingly important for our overall well-being. Building and sustaining relationships not only provides a sense of belonging and support but also contributes to our emotional, mental, and physical health. Nurturing meaningful relationships involves intentional efforts to connect with others, develop deep bonds, and cultivate a supportive community. By practicing strategies that enhance connection, individuals can experience the profound benefits that come from building and sustaining meaningful relationships.

"The bond that links your true family is not one of blood, but of respect and joy in each other's life."

– Richard Bach

Active Listening and Empathy

- Engage in active listening by giving full attention to others and seeking to understand their perspectives.

- Practice empathy by putting yourself in the shoes of others and validating their emotions.

- Show genuine interest in others' experiences and actively engage in conversations.

- Offer support and understanding without judgment.

Authenticity and Vulnerability

- Be authentic and genuine in your interactions, allowing others to see the real you.

- Share your thoughts, feelings, and experiences openly and honestly.

- Create a safe space for others to express themselves and share their vulnerabilities.

- Foster a culture of trust and acceptance within your relationships.

Regular Communication and Quality Time

- Maintain regular communication with loved ones, friends, and community members.

- Make time for meaningful interactions and quality conversations.

- Use various communication channels, including in-person meetings, phone calls, video chats, and written messages.

- Prioritise spending quality time together and engage in activities that strengthen the bond.

Acts of Kindness and Support

- Practice random acts of kindness to show care and support for others.

- Offer help and support when needed, expecting nothing in return.

- Celebrate others' successes and milestones and be there for them during challenging times.

- Engage in collaborative efforts and contribute to the well-being of your community.

Shared Interests and Activities

- Explore shared interests and engage in activities together.

- Join clubs, groups, or communities centred around common hobbies, passions, or causes.

- Participate in events, workshops, or gatherings where you can connect with like-minded individuals.

- Foster a sense of belonging and connection through shared experiences.

Respect and Acceptance

- Show respect for diversity and embrace differences in opinions, beliefs, and backgrounds.

- Practice active inclusivity and create an environment where everyone feels valued and accepted.

- Avoid judgment and criticism and instead focus on understanding and learning from others.

- Foster a culture of respect and acceptance within your relationships and community.

By actively incorporating these strategies into our lives, we can nurture and sustain meaningful connections. Building and maintaining relationships requires time, effort, and commitment, but the rewards are immense. Meaningful connections bring joy, support, and a sense of belonging, enhancing our overall well-being and contributing to a happier, more fulfilling life.

COMMUNITY POWER: INSPIRING PERSONAL STORIES

Elon Musk

Born in 1971 in South Africa, Elon Musk is a renowned entrepreneur and innovator known for his groundbreaking ventures such as Tesla, SpaceX, and Neuralink.

Elon Musk's personal story exemplifies the power of the community in achieving extraordinary goals. Through his various ventures, Musk has rallied communities of scientists, engineers, and enthusiasts who share his vision for a sustainable future and space exploration. He has actively involved the public in his ventures, encouraging participation and collaboration to drive innovation.

Musk's approach to building a community extends beyond his business endeavours. He actively engages with his followers on social media platforms, fostering a sense of connection and dialogue. Musk's open-source approach to technology, such as making Tesla's patents available to the public, demonstrates his belief in the power of collective knowledge and collaboration.

Through his relentless pursuit of ambitious goals and his ability to inspire and mobilise communities, Elon Musk showcases the transformative potential of harnessing the power of the community. His story serves as an inspiration for individuals to come together, share ideas, and work collaboratively to overcome challenges and create a better future.

Dwayne Johnson

Dwayne Johnson, also known as "The Rock," is a well-known actor, producer, and former professional wrestler. Throughout his life, Johnson has emphasised the importance of connection and community in his journey towards a positive life. He has openly shared his experiences and the role that others have played in supporting and encouraging him. Johnson grew up in a family with a strong wrestling background, and his father, Rocky Johnson, was a professional wrestler. Despite having a challenging childhood and facing financial struggles, Johnson found solace in the wrestling community. He recognised the power of connection and the support he received from his peers and mentors. Johnson once stated, *"I had mentors who believed in me and saw potential in me even when I didn't see it in myself."* As he pursued his career in professional wrestling and later transitioned into acting, Johnson maintained a strong sense of community. He actively engaged with his fans, recognising their importance in his success. He used social media platforms to connect with his followers, sharing personal stories, motivating messages, and encouraging them to pursue their dreams. Through his interactions, Johnson emphasised the significance of supporting one another and fostering positive connections. Johnson's journey of connection and community taught him valuable lessons. He learned that success is not solely an individual achievement but a result of the support and encouragement from others. He once said, *"Success isn't always about greatness. It's about consistency. Consistent hard work leads to success. Greatness will come."*

Johnson's story highlights the transformative power of connection and the positive impact it can have on one's life. His journey reminds us of the importance of building meaningful relationships, seeking support from others, and embracing the power of community.

Oprah Winfrey

Oprah Winfrey, a renowned media mogul, philanthropist, and influential figure, has spoken extensively about the power of connection and community in transforming her life and achieving a positive mindset. She emphasises the importance of surrounding oneself with uplifting and supportive individuals who contribute to personal growth and well-being. In her own words, Oprah shares, *"Surround yourself with only people who are going to lift you higher"* (Winfrey, 2006). Oprah's journey of connection and community began when she started building her network of mentors, friends, and collaborators who shared her vision and supported her aspirations. She recognised that by surrounding herself with positive influences, she could overcome challenges, cultivate resilience, and thrive. Through her talk show, "The Oprah Winfrey Show," Oprah connected with millions of people worldwide, creating a community of individuals who felt inspired and empowered by her stories and teachings. She encouraged her audience to engage in open dialogue, share their experiences, and create a sense of belonging.

Subhash Chandra Bose

Born in 1897 in India, Bose was a charismatic leader and freedom fighter during the Indian independence movement. He believed that collective action and the strength of the community were essential in achieving freedom for India.

Bose recognised the power of unity and organised various community-driven initiatives to fight against British colonial rule. One of his notable contributions was the formation of the Forward Bloc, a political organisation aimed at uniting like-minded individuals and galvanising them into action. He believed that by fostering a sense of community and instilling a shared purpose, the movement for independence would gain momentum.

Subhash Chandra Bose also understood the significance of international cooperation and community building. He sought support from different countries and forged alliances with leaders and communities across the globe to advance the cause of Indian independence. By harnessing the power of communities, both within India and beyond its borders, Bose created a formidable force that challenged the oppressive rule of the British Empire.

Bose's commitment to community empowerment and his ability to mobilise people towards a common goal serve as an inspiring example of how individuals can harness the power of the community to bring about significant change. His legacy continues to remind us of the transformative potential that lies within a united community, working together for a shared purpose.

9
LIVING WITH PURPOSE

"The meaning of life is not found in what happens to you but in what you make of it."

— Viktor Frankl

L iving a life filled with purpose is a powerful way to cultivate positive energy and experience a deep sense of fulfilment. When we have a clear sense of purpose, our actions and choices align with our values and beliefs, leading to a greater sense of meaning and satisfaction in life. In this section, we will explore the importance of living with purpose, what it means to have a purpose-driven life, and how it promotes the cultivation of positive energy.

What is *'purpose'*? Purpose can be defined as the underlying reason or motivation behind our actions and existence. It is the sense of direction and meaning that drives us to pursue specific goals and contribute to something greater than ourselves. Purpose goes beyond mere survival and encompasses our values, passions, and aspirations. A purpose-driven life is one in which our actions and choices are guided by our deepest values and intentions. It involves aligning our daily activities with our larger life purpose. When we live with purpose, we have a clear understanding of what matters most to us, and we consciously shape our lives around those principles. Purpose-driven individuals are driven by a sense of mission, and their actions are fuelled by passion and a desire to make a positive impact on the world.

Living with purpose promotes and cultivates positive energy in various ways. Foremost, having a sense of purpose gives us a reason to wake up every morning with enthusiasm and determination. It provides a sense of direction and a clear focus, which in turn fuels our motivation and energy levels. When we know that our actions are contributing to something meaningful, we are more likely to approach each day with a sense of purpose and vitality. Furthermore, living with purpose brings a deep sense of fulfilment and satisfaction. It allows us to tap into our unique strengths and talents, enabling us to make a meaningful difference in our own lives and the lives of others. When we engage in activities that align with our purpose, we experience a state of flow—an optimal psychological state characterised by intense focus, enjoyment, and a sense of timelessness. This flow state not only enhances our overall well-being but also amplifies our positive energy. Living with purpose also fosters resilience and provides a source of motivation during challenging times. When we encounter obstacles or setbacks, having a clear sense of purpose helps us navigate through difficulties with greater resilience and determination. Our purpose acts as an anchor, reminding us of the bigger picture and inspiring us to persevere, even in the face of adversity.

IDENTIFY YOUR UNIQUE PURPOSE

In my own journey, I have discovered the transformative power of living with purpose. By identifying my core values and aligning my actions with them, I have experienced a profound shift in my energy and overall well-being. Every day, I remind myself of my purpose, and it serves as a guiding light, motivating me to take meaningful steps towards my goals and make a positive impact in the lives of others. Remember, your purpose is unique to you. Embrace it, live it, and let it fuel your positive energy as you make a meaningful impact on the world.

As Viktor Frankl once said, "Those who have a 'why' to live can bear with almost any 'how'." Having a clear purpose gives our lives depth and meaning, enabling us to cultivate positive energy and live with a greater sense of fulfilment. In the following sections, we will delve deeper into the process of discovering and living with purpose, providing practical strategies and insights to help you embark on your own purpose-driven journey. Living a purposeful life has the remarkable ability to cultivate and spread positive energy not only within ourselves, but also to those around us. It is through living with a sense of purpose that we tap into our full potential, find deep fulfilment, and inspire others to do the same. In this section, we will explore the transformative power of living a purposeful life and how it influences our energy and the energy of others. Rick Warren, a renowned pastor and author, emphasises the significance of living with purpose by stating, *"You were made by God and for God, and until you understand that, life will never make sense."* This profound insight highlights the connection between purpose and a sense of meaning in life. When we discover our purpose and align our actions with it, we experience a greater sense of coherence and fulfilment. Our energy becomes focused, purpose-driven, and aligned with our deepest values.

Brené Brown explains that *"Authenticity is the daily practice of letting go of who we think we're supposed to be and embracing who we are."* Living a purposeful life requires us to be authentic to ourselves. When we live in alignment with our purpose, we embody our authentic selves, and this authenticity radiates positive energy to those around us. Our genuine enthusiasm and passion inspire others to embrace their own purpose and live authentically. Meanwhile, Viktor Frankl, in his seminal work "Man's Search for Meaning," posits that *"The meaning of life is not found in what happens to you but in what you make of it."* This perspective underscores the transformative power of purpose. Regardless of our circumstances, living with purpose empowers us to make meaning out of our experiences. It allows us to channel our energy into activities that align with our purpose, turning challenges into opportunities for growth and transformation. According to Mihaly Csikszentmihalyi, a purposeful life brings us into a state of flow, where our skills and challenges are in perfect harmony. In this state, our energy is fully engaged, and we experience a deep sense of joy, fulfilment, and positive energy. By embracing our purpose, we create a pathway to accessing this state of flow more consistently. As we live with purpose, our positive energy has a ripple effect on others. Our purpose-driven actions inspire and motivate those around us to pursue their own passions and live authentically. By sharing our purpose and inviting others to align their actions with their own values and dreams, we create a supportive community that fosters positive energy. This interconnectedness amplifies the impact of our individual purposes and enables us to collectively create a more positive and purposeful world.

In my own life, I have witnessed the transformative power of living with purpose. By embracing my purpose and aligning my actions with my deepest values, I have experienced a profound shift in my energy and outlook. The positive energy I radiate has touched the lives of those around me, creating a ripple effect of inspiration and empowerment.

Living a purposeful life is a continuous journey of self-discovery, growth, and contribution. It requires introspection, courage, and a commitment to living in alignment with our values. As we embrace our purpose, we unleash a wellspring of positive energy within ourselves and become catalysts for positive change in the world. T.D. Jakes, a renowned pastor and author once said: *"If you can't figure out your purpose, figure out your passion. For your passion will lead you right into your purpose."* Embrace your passions, discover your purpose, and let the power of a purposeful life guide you in cultivating and spreading positive energy to create a brighter and more meaningful existence for yourself and others.

TECHNIQUES FOR DISCOVERING YOUR PURPOSE

Discovering your purpose is a profound and transformative journey that can bring immense fulfilment and contribute to cultivating positive energy in your life. Here are some key techniques supported by experts to help you uncover your purpose:

Reflect on Your Values and Passions

In his book "The Purpose Driven Life", Rick Warren says, *"Knowing your purpose in life is not about guessing or wishing; it's about discovering what matters to you and what you care about deeply."* Take time to reflect on your values and passions. This self-reflection can guide you toward a purpose that aligns with who you are at your core (Warren, 2002). Barbara Fredrickson suggests incorporating self-reflection exercises into your daily routine. These may include writing in a journal, practicing mindfulness, or engaging in creative activities that encourage introspection. These exercises can help you connect with your inner self and uncover insights about your purpose (Fredrickson, 2004).

Consider Your Strengths and Skills

Viktor Frankl said in his book "Man's Search for Meaning," that our purpose often lies in utilising our unique strengths and skills to make a difference. Reflect on what you excel at and enjoy doing. By aligning your purpose with your natural abilities, you can create a powerful impact (Frankl, 1946).

Seek Inspiration from Others

Seeking inspiration from individuals who have already discovered their purpose. Engage in conversations with people you admire and learn about their journeys. Their insights and experiences can provide valuable guidance on finding your own purpose (Jimenez, Hoffman, & Grant, 2011). Seek guidance from a mentor or coach.

Embrace Experimentation

According to Mihaly Csikszentmihalyi, the renowned psychologist, experimentation plays a crucial role in discovering purpose. Try new activities, explore different interests, and step outside your comfort zone. Through these experiences, you can gain clarity about what truly resonates with you and find your sense of purpose (Csikszentmihalyi, 1990).

Embrace the Growth Mindset

Embrace the belief that your abilities can be developed through dedication and hard work. This mindset allows you to view challenges as opportunities for growth and helps you navigate the journey of purpose with resilience and determination (Dweck, 2006).

Embrace the Process

John Ortberg reminds us that discovering our purpose is not an overnight endeavour. It requires patience and a willingness to embrace the process. Allow yourself the space to explore and learn, and trust that your purpose will unfold organically (Ortberg, 2014).

Recall, the process of discovering your purpose is personal and unique to you. It may involve moments of self-reflection, exploration, and even uncertainty. As you embark on this journey, consider the words of Jane Dutton, a renowned positive organisational psychologist: *"Living a purposeful life is not about finding a single answer; it's about cultivating a sense of direction and continually evolving your purpose over time"* (Dutton, 2003).

THE IMPACT OF LIVING WITH PURPOSE ON MENTAL & EMOTIONAL WELL-BEING

In a world bustling with distractions and demands, it is all too easy to lose sight of our true purpose and the profound impact it can have on our mental and emotional well-being. The quest for a meaningful and purposeful life is not merely an abstract concept; it is a powerful force that has the potential to transform our inner landscape. When we live with purpose, a remarkable transformation occurs within us, guiding our thoughts, actions, and decisions with unwavering clarity. The impact of living with purpose on our mental and emotional well-being is nothing short of astounding, as it ignites a flame of fulfilment, resilience, and authenticity that reverberates through every fibre of our being. In this journey of exploration, we will delve into the depths of this transformative power, unravelling the threads that weave purpose into the tapestry of our lives and discovering the profound effects it has on our mental and emotional well-being.

Enhancing Mental Health

Living with purpose has a profound impact on mental health. When individuals have a clear sense of purpose, it provides them with a sense of direction and meaning in their lives. This clarity helps alleviate feelings of confusion and uncertainty, reducing stress and anxiety. Moreover, having a purpose provides a framework for decision-making, enabling individuals to prioritise their goals and make choices aligned with their values. This alignment promotes a sense of authenticity and boosts self-esteem, leading to improved mental well-being.

Living with purpose also contributes to a stronger sense of identity and self-worth. When individuals have a clear purpose, they have a deeper understanding of their strengths, passions, and values. This self-awareness fosters a positive self-image and self-acceptance, reducing self-doubt and negative self-talk. As a result, individuals experience increased confidence, self-assurance, and a greater sense of overall well-being.

Cultivating Emotional Resilience

Living with purpose equips individuals with the tools to navigate life's challenges and setbacks more effectively. Having a sense of purpose provides a sense of resilience, allowing individuals to bounce back from adversity and maintain a positive outlook. When faced with difficulties, individuals with a clear purpose can draw upon their sense of meaning and motivation to persevere. This resilience helps them cope with stress, overcome obstacles, and maintain emotional well-being.

Living with purpose also fosters a sense of fulfilment and satisfaction. When individuals are actively engaged in activities and pursuits aligned with their purpose, they experience a greater sense of joy, fulfilment, and passion. This sense of fulfilment acts as a buffer against negative emotions, providing individuals with a greater capacity to handle stress and maintain emotional balance. As a result, individuals are better equipped to cope with life's challenges, experience positive emotions, and maintain overall emotional well-being.

In conclusion, living with purpose has a profound impact on mental and emotional well-being. It enhances mental health by providing clarity, reducing stress, and promoting self-esteem. It also cultivates emotional resilience by fostering a positive outlook, enabling individuals to navigate challenges effectively. By incorporating purpose into their lives, individuals experience greater fulfilment, joy, and a stronger sense of identity. The journey of living with purpose not only contributes to improved mental and emotional well-being but also enables individuals to lead more meaningful and fulfilling lives.

THE ROLE OF GRATITUDE IN LIVING A PURPOSEFUL LIFE

Gratitude is the practice of acknowledging and appreciating the positive aspects of life, both big and small. When incorporated into our daily lives, gratitude can significantly enhance our sense of purpose and overall well-being.

Below are some key aspects to consider when examining the role of gratitude in living a purposeful life:

- **Cultivating Appreciation:** Gratitude allows us to recognise and appreciate the abundance and blessings in our lives. By shifting our focus from what is lacking to what we already have, we develop a sense of contentment and fulfilment.

- **Aligning with Values:** Gratitude helps us align our actions and choices with our core values. When we acknowledge the positive aspects of our lives, we become more attuned to what truly matters to us, making it easier to live in alignment with our purpose.

- **Perspective Shift:** Practicing gratitude encourages us to adopt a positive perspective and see challenges as opportunities for growth. It helps us reframe setbacks and difficulties, allowing us to approach them with resilience and optimism.

- **Connection and Compassion:** Gratitude promotes a deeper sense of connection with others and fosters empathy and compassion. By recognising the contributions and support of those around us, we strengthen our relationships and find greater fulfilment in our interactions.

- **Sustaining Motivation:** Gratitude acts as a powerful motivator, fuelling our drive to pursue our purpose and make a positive impact in the world. It helps us stay focused, inspired, and committed to our goals, even in the face of challenges.

By incorporating gratitude into our daily lives, we can enhance our sense of purpose, leading to greater fulfilment, joy, and overall well-being.

PURSUIT OF PURPOSE: PERSONAL STORIES OF FULFILMENT & JOY

In this section, we will embark on a journey inspired by the personal stories of individuals who have discovered true fulfilment and joy through living with purpose. Through these narratives, we will delve deeper into the pivotal moments, challenges faced, and lessons learned by these remarkable individuals.

Rick Warren

Rick Warren's journey towards purpose began with a profound spiritual awakening. As a young pastor, he felt a calling to make a difference in people's lives. Through introspection and prayer, he identified the central purpose of his existence: to love God and love people unconditionally. This revelation became the guiding light that shaped his actions, decisions, and ministry.

Rick Warren's purpose-driven life led him to establish Saddleback Church, a community-centred congregation that strives to meet the physical, emotional, and spiritual needs of its members. He initiated several outreach programs and humanitarian efforts, including programs to combat poverty, provide healthcare, and support education.

Warren's story teaches us the significance of aligning our purpose with our love for others and our desire to serve. It reminds us that true fulfilment lies in selfless acts of kindness and making a positive impact in the lives of those around us.

Brené Brown

Brené Brown's personal journey towards purpose began with a deep exploration of vulnerability and shame. Through her research, she discovered that embracing vulnerability and practicing courage were integral to living a wholehearted life. Her own struggles with vulnerability became a catalyst for her work and a source of inspiration for millions of individuals around the world. Brown's vulnerability and authenticity have resonated with people from all walks of life. Through her books, TED Talks, and workshops, she encourages others to embrace their imperfections and lead lives guided by courage and compassion. Her story exemplifies the transformative power of living authentically and cultivating meaningful connections with others.

Brown's journey teaches us the importance of embracing vulnerability as a gateway to personal growth, resilience, and wholehearted living. It reminds us that by embracing our own imperfections, we can create spaces where others feel seen, heard, and valued.

Viktor Frankl

Viktor Frankl's story is one of resilience and finding meaning in the midst of unimaginable suffering. As a psychiatrist and Holocaust survivor, Frankl experienced the depths of human cruelty and despair. However, it was during his time in concentration camps that he made a remarkable discovery: the power of finding meaning and purpose in life, even in the most challenging circumstances. Frankl realised that those who had a sense of purpose and a "why" to live could find strength and endure any hardship. He recognised that purpose is not dictated by external circumstances, but is something deeply personal and unique to each individual. His experiences led him to develop logotherapy, a therapeutic approach focused on helping individuals find meaning in life.

Frankl's story serves as a powerful reminder that even in the darkest times, we can choose to find purpose and meaning. It urges us to reflect on our own lives and seek a deeper understanding of our values and aspirations, so we can live with intention and make a positive impact on the world.

Mihaly Csikszentmihalyi

Mihaly Csikszentmihalyi's journey towards understanding purpose led him to explore the concept of "flow" and its connection to happiness and fulfilment. Through his research, he discovered that people experience the highest levels of engagement and joy when they are fully immersed in activities that align with their skills and interests. Csikszentmihalyi's own experiences with flow, a state of optimal experience, drove him to delve deeper into understanding the conditions that foster it. He found that when individuals engage in activities that challenge their skills while providing a sense of purpose and enjoyment, they enter a state of flow characterised by deep focus, satisfaction, and personal growth. His story reminds us of the importance of aligning our passions, skills, and goals to discover activities that bring us joy and a profound sense of purpose. It encourages us to seek moments of flow in our lives and find endeavours that allow us to tap into our full potential.

Through these personal stories, we embark on a journey of self-discovery and inspiration. Each narrative offers valuable insights and lessons, urging us to reflect on our own values, passions, and aspirations. By aligning our actions with a sense of purpose, we can experience true fulfilment, spread positive energy, and make a meaningful impact on the world around us.

A. P. J. Abdul Kalam

A. P. J. Abdul Kalam's personal story is an inspiring example of finding fulfilment and joy through living with purpose. Known as the "People's President" and a renowned scientist, Kalam dedicated his life to serving his nation and inspiring future generations.

Kalam's journey was marked by his unwavering commitment to scientific research and innovation. His work in aerospace engineering earned him many accolades and respect from his peers. However, he believed that true fulfilment came not just from personal achievements, but from using his knowledge and expertise to benefit society.

As the President of India from 2002 to 2007, Kalam embraced his role as a statesman and a visionary leader. He focused on igniting the minds of young individuals and encouraging them to pursue their dreams. Kalam travelled extensively across the country, engaging with students and inspiring them with his words of wisdom. He believed that by empowering the youth and nurturing their potential, India could achieve greatness.

Kalam's personal mantra of "Dream, Dream, Dream" resonated deeply with people of all ages. He emphasised the importance of having a purpose and setting ambitious goals, while also encouraging individuals to work hard and persevere in the face of challenges. Kalam's infectious enthusiasm and genuine passion for making a difference touched the lives of millions, leaving a lasting impact on generations to come.

Through his personal story, A. P. J. Abdul Kalam exemplifies the profound fulfilment and joy that comes from living a life of purpose. His dedication to serving humanity and inspiring others serves as an inspiration for individuals to find their own path of purpose, contributing to the betterment of society and finding true happiness.

10
MAINTAINING A POSITIVE LIFE

"The only thing that stands between you and your dream is the will to try and the belief that it is actually possible."

Joel Brown

Living a positive life is not just a fleeting experience but a lifelong commitment to cultivating happiness, well-being, and fulfilment. Throughout this book, we have explored the power of positivity and its impact on our thoughts, emotions, relationships, and overall quality of life. Now, let us delve deeper into the essence of maintaining a sustainable, positive life in all its facets. The journey towards a positive life begins with the mind. It is in our thoughts that the seeds of positivity are sown, and it is through our thoughts that we shape our reality. As Ralph Waldo Emerson once said, *"The mind is everything. What you think, you become."* It is essential to nurture a positive mindset that empowers and uplifts us. We have the ability to choose our thoughts and to reframe them into positive and empowering narratives. By embracing optimism, self-belief, and gratitude, we invite positivity to permeate our consciousness and shape our experiences.

Positive self-talk is also a powerful tool that helps us cultivate a nurturing inner dialogue. Steve Maraboli beautifully captures its essence, stating, *"The more you practise positive self-talk, the more you will believe in yourself and the more likely you are to achieve your goals."* By consciously and intentionally speaking to ourselves with kindness, encouragement, and self-compassion, we foster a strong sense of self-esteem and self-confidence. We become our own cheerleaders, supporting and motivating ourselves even in the face of challenges.

However, maintaining a positive life extends beyond our internal dialogue. Our relationships play a significant role in our overall well-being. Surrounding ourselves with positive influences and cultivating uplifting connections is essential. As we interact with others, let us remember the words of Maya Angelou, who said, *"People will forget what you said, people will forget what you did, but people will never forget how you made them feel."* By practicing empathy, kindness, and compassion, we create a ripple effect of positivity that spreads to those around us. Our genuine care and support can have a profound impact on the lives of others, making a positive difference in our communities and the world. To maintain a sustainable positive life, we must also pay attention to our lifestyle choices. Engaging in self-care activities that nourish our mind, body, and soul is vital. It is through self-care that we replenish our energy and restore our inner balance. As we prioritise self-care, we honour ourselves and acknowledge our worthiness of love, care, and rejuvenation.

Creating a positive physical environment is equally important. The colours, designs, and arrangements in our spaces can greatly influence our mood and overall well-being. As we surround ourselves with vibrant colours, natural elements, and meaningful objects, we invite positive energy into our surroundings. The famous architect Frank Lloyd Wright once said, *"Space is the breath of art",* reminding us of the power of a well-designed space to evoke inspiration, tranquillity, and positivity.

Cultivating positivity is not a one-time achievement; it requires ongoing effort, commitment, and a genuine desire to prioritise your well-being. By implementing these tips into your daily routine, you can create a solid foundation for a life filled with joy, resilience, and purpose.

In my own personal journey, maintaining a positive life has been a transformative process. I used to find myself overwhelmed by negativity and the pressures of daily life. However, through self-reflection and the implementation of these strategies, I have experienced a significant shift in my mindset and overall well-being.

By practicing gratitude, I discovered the power of appreciating the small blessings in my life and shifting my focus to the positive aspects. Surrounding myself with positive influences has been instrumental in creating a supportive network that uplifts and inspires me. Engaging in self-care has allowed me to prioritise my needs and recharge my energy.

Embracing resilience has helped me navigate through challenges with a sense of determination and optimism. Finding meaning and purpose has given me a greater sense of direction and fulfilment. Mindfulness has allowed me to be more present and fully enjoy each moment.

By maintaining healthy boundaries, I have learned to protect my well-being and focus on activities that align with my values and goals. Celebrating progress has taught me the importance of self-compassion and appreciating the growth I have made, no matter how small.

Through this personal journey, I have come to realise that maintaining a positive life is a continuous process. It requires commitment, self-reflection, and a willingness to prioritise my well-being. By embracing these strategies, I have experienced a profound transformation and a newfound sense of joy, purpose, and fulfilment.

As you embark on your own journey towards a positive life, remember that it is within your reach. By implementing these tips, learning from the experiences of others, and nurturing your own growth, you can create a life filled with positivity, resilience, and fulfilment.

Repeat affirmations such as "I am capable of overcoming challenges" or "I embrace joy and gratitude at every moment." This simple practice sets the tone for a positive mindset and helps you navigate the day with confidence. Psychologist T.D. Jakes emphasises, *"You can change your world by changing your words."*

Disconnect from Negativity. Limit exposure to negative influences, whether it's news, social media, or toxic relationships. Surround yourself with positive and uplifting content that nourishes your mind and soul. Set boundaries to protect your well-being and prioritise activities that bring you joy and fulfilment. As motivational speaker Les Brown advises, "*Surround yourself with positive people who believe in your dreams, encourage your ideas, support your ambitions, and bring out the best in you.*"

NURTURING POSITIVE RELATIONSHIPS: THE POWER OF CONNECTION

In a world where connections have become more crucial than ever, nurturing positive relationships holds the key to a fulfilling and joyful life. The power of connection transcends boundaries and enriches our experiences, bringing warmth, support, and a sense of belonging. When we prioritise cultivating positive relationships, we open ourselves up to a world of possibilities where understanding, empathy, and shared experiences flourish. Whether it is with family, friends, colleagues, or even strangers, every connection we foster has the potential to shape our lives in profound ways. By exploring the power of connection and delving into personal stories of individuals who have embraced this transformative force, we embark on a journey to unlock the beauty and depth of human connections, ultimately discovering the immense positive impact they can have on our lives.

Significance of Positive Relationships in maintaining a Positive Life

Positive relationships are the lifeblood of our well-being and play a crucial role in maintaining a positive life. Let's explore the significance of positive relationships and how they contribute to our overall happiness and fulfilment:

- **Emotional Support and Encouragement:** Positive relationships provide us with a support system that is essential for navigating life's ups and downs. When we have people who genuinely care about our well-being, they become a source of emotional support, offering a listening ear, words of encouragement, and empathy. They help us see the silver linings in challenging situations and inspire us to keep moving forward.

- **Boost in Mental Health:** Building and nurturing positive relationships can have a profound impact on our mental health. Engaging in meaningful connections reduces feelings of loneliness, isolation, and depression. It creates a sense of belonging and purpose, fostering a positive mindset and enhancing overall well-being. Sharing our joys, sorrows, and experiences with trusted individuals cultivates a sense of validation, self-worth, and resilience.

- **Personal Growth and Development:** Positive relationships provide a fertile ground for personal growth and development. They serve as mirrors, reflecting our strengths and areas for improvement. Supportive individuals challenge us to step out of our comfort zones, pursue our passions, and unleash our full potential. Through constructive feedback, mentorship, and guidance, they help us learn and evolve, leading to continuous self-improvement.

- **Increased Happiness and Life Satisfaction:** When we surround ourselves with positive relationships, we experience greater happiness and life satisfaction. Genuine connections bring joy, laughter, and shared experiences into our lives. They create a sense of belonging, acceptance, and love, which are fundamental human needs. By fostering positive relationships, we create a positive feedback loop, where happiness and positivity are nurtured and amplified.

- **Stress Reduction and Resilience:** Positive relationships act as a buffer against stress and adversity. When faced with challenges, having a strong support system can help us manage stress effectively. The emotional and practical support from loved ones reduces the burden and provides a sense of relief. Moreover, positive relationships provide a safe space where we can share our concerns and seek guidance, allowing us to bounce back from setbacks and build resilience.

In conclusion, positive relationships are not just a source of happiness, but also a critical ingredient in maintaining a positive life. They provide emotional support, foster mental well-being, promote personal growth, enhance happiness, and build resilience. Nurturing and investing in these relationships is an investment in our overall well-being and the key to leading a fulfilling and positive life.

Strategies for Cultivating and Nurturing Meaningful Connections

Developing and nurturing meaningful connections is essential for creating a fulfilling and enriching life. Cultivating deep and genuine relationships requires intention, effort, and a willingness to invest in the well-being of others. Here are some strategies for cultivating and nurturing meaningful connections:

- **Active Listening:** One of the most important strategies for cultivating meaningful connections is to practise active listening. Truly listening to others, without interrupting or judging, demonstrates respect and empathy. It shows that you value their thoughts, feelings, and experiences. By giving your full attention and being present in conversations, you create a safe space for open and honest communication.

- **Authenticity and Vulnerability:** Authenticity is the foundation of meaningful connections. Being genuine and true to yourself allows others to connect with the real you. Embracing vulnerability by sharing your thoughts, fears, and aspirations creates a deeper level of trust and intimacy. When you open up and show vulnerability, it encourages others to do the same, fostering a sense of connection and understanding.

- **Cultivating Empathy:** Empathy is the ability to understand and share the feelings of others. Cultivating empathy involves putting yourself in someone else's shoes and seeking to understand their perspective and emotions. It requires active compassion and a willingness to listen without judgment. By practicing empathy, you demonstrate care and support, deepening your connections with others.

- **Regular Communication and Quality Time:** Meaningful connections require regular communication and quality time together. Make an effort to stay in touch, whether through phone calls, video chats, or in-person meetings. Show interest in their lives, ask about their well-being, and celebrate their successes. Create opportunities to spend quality time together, engaging in activities that bring joy and foster connection.

- **Support and Encouragement:** Being a source of support and encouragement strengthens meaningful connections. Offer a helping hand when needed, provide emotional support during challenging times, and celebrate achievements together. Show genuine interest in their goals and dreams, and cheer them on along their journey. Being a supportive presence in someone's life deepens the bond and creates a sense of trust.

- **Shared Experience and Creating Memories:** Meaningful connections are often built through shared experiences and creating lasting memories. Engage in activities together, such as travelling, volunteering, or pursuing common interests. These shared experiences create bonds and provide opportunities for deeper connection and understanding.

- **Gratitude and Appreciation:** Expressing gratitude and appreciation towards others is a powerful way to nurture meaningful connections. Acknowledge and thank them for their presence in your life, their support, and the positive impact they have on you. Small gestures of appreciation, such as sending a heartfelt note or expressing gratitude in person, strengthen the bond and reinforce the value you place on the relationship.

In conclusion, cultivating and nurturing meaningful connections requires active effort, empathy, and authenticity. By practicing active listening, embracing vulnerability, cultivating empathy, maintaining regular communication, providing support, creating shared experiences, and expressing gratitude, you can cultivate deep and meaningful relationships that enrich your life and the lives of those around you.

SELF-CARE & WELL-BEING PRACTICES: SUSTAINING POSITIVE ENERGY

Self-care and well-being practices are essential for sustaining positive energy in our lives. It involves nurturing and prioritising our physical, mental, and emotional health, allowing us to recharge, restore balance, and cultivate a strong foundation of positive energy. By engaging in self-care activities such as regular exercise, healthy eating, mindfulness practices, and adequate rest, we can enhance our overall well-being and maintain a positive mindset. Taking time for self-care not only replenishes our energy reserves, but also equips us with the resilience and strength needed to navigate life's challenges with a positive outlook. Through these practices, we can sustain our positive energy and foster a sense of well-being, ultimately leading to a more fulfilled and vibrant life.

The Role of Self-Care in Maintaining Positive Energy and Well-Being

Self-care plays a crucial role in maintaining positive energy and overall well-being. It involves taking intentional actions to nurture and prioritise our physical, mental, and emotional health. By incorporating self-care practices into our daily lives, we can effectively replenish our energy reserves, reduce stress, and enhance our overall sense of well-being. Here are some key aspects and strategies that highlight the role of self-care in maintaining positive energy:

- **Physical Well-Being:** Taking care of our physical health is essential for sustaining positive energy. This includes engaging in regular exercise, eating nutritious meals, getting enough sleep, and practicing relaxation techniques. Prioritising physical well-being not only boosts our energy levels but also promotes a sense of vitality and overall wellness.

- **Mental and Emotional Well-Being:** Self-care is vital for maintaining optimal mental and emotional health. It involves practicing mindfulness, engaging in activities that bring joy and relaxation, seeking support when needed, and setting boundaries to protect our mental and emotional space. These practices help reduce stress, enhance self-awareness, and cultivate a positive mindset.

- **Self-Reflection and Inner Growth:** Self-care provides an opportunity for self-reflection and personal growth. Setting aside time for introspection, journaling, or engaging in activities that foster self-discovery can help us better understand ourselves, identify our needs and desires, and align our actions with our values. This process of self-reflection contributes to a deeper sense of self-compassion and personal growth, leading to increased positive energy.

- **Establishing Healthy Boundaries:** Self-care involves setting boundaries to protect our energy and well-being. This includes learning to say no when necessary, prioritising our needs, and creating a healthy work-life balance. By establishing healthy boundaries, we can avoid burnout, maintain a sense of control over our lives, and preserve our positive energy.

- **Cultivating Mindfulness and Gratitude:** Practicing mindfulness and gratitude are powerful self-care strategies that help us stay present, appreciate the small joys in life, and cultivate a positive outlook. Mindfulness techniques, such as meditation or deep breathing exercises, can help reduce stress and promote inner calm. Expressing gratitude for the blessings in our lives shifts our focus towards the positive aspects, fostering a sense of contentment and increasing our overall positive energy.

Incorporating these self-care practices into our daily routines empowers us to maintain positive energy and well-being. It is essential to remember that self-care is not selfish but rather a necessary investment in our own health and happiness. By prioritising self-care, we can sustain positive energy, nurture our well-being, and navigate life with a renewed sense of vitality and positivity.

Effective Self-Care Practices for Nurturing Mind, Body, and Soul

Taking care of our mind, body, and soul is essential for maintaining overall well-being and cultivating positive energy. Here are some effective self-care practices that can help nurture these aspects of our being:

Mind

- **Practice Mindfulness:** Engage in activities that promote present-moment awareness, such as meditation, deep breathing exercises, or mindful walking. This helps calm the mind, reduce stress, and increase mental clarity.

- **Prioritise Mental Breaks:** Schedule regular breaks throughout the day to rest and recharge.

This could involve stepping away from work, engaging in a hobby, or simply taking a few moments for quiet reflection.

- **Engage in Creative Pursuits:** Explore activities that stimulate creativity and bring joy, such as painting, writing, playing a musical instrument, or dancing. These outlets allow for self-expression and can be deeply therapeutic for the mind.

Body

- **Move Your Body:** Engage in regular physical activity that you enjoy, such as walking, jogging, yoga, or dancing. Physical exercise not only benefits your physical health but also boosts mood and energy levels.

- **Nourish Yourself with Healthy Foods:** Prioritise a balanced diet that includes plenty of fruits, vegetables, whole grains, and lean proteins. Pay attention to your body's nutritional needs and fuel yourself with nourishing foods.

- **Get Enough Restorative Sleep:** Establish a consistent sleep routine that allows for adequate rest. Create a calming sleep environment, practice relaxation techniques before bed, and ensure you prioritise sufficient sleep each night.

Soul

- **Connect with Nature:** Spend time outdoors and immerse yourself in nature. Whether it's going for a walk in the park, gardening, or simply sitting under a tree, connecting with nature can provide a sense of peace and rejuvenation.

- **Engage in Activities that bring Joy:** Identify activities or hobbies that bring you joy and make time for them regularly. It could be reading, listening to music, practicing a craft, or spending time with loved ones.

- **Cultivate a Gratitude Practice:** Take time each day to reflect on the things you are grateful for. This practice shifts your focus to the positive aspects of life and helps foster a sense of contentment and appreciation.

Remember, self-care is a personal journey, and it's important to find practices that resonate with you. The key is to prioritise self-care as a non-negotiable part of your routine and listen to your mind, body, and soul's needs. By nurturing these aspects of yourself, you can cultivate positive energy, enhance well-being, and lead a more fulfilling life.

FINDING MEANING AND PURPOSE IN EVERYDAY LIFE

Finding meaning and purpose in our everyday lives is a transformative journey that can bring depth, fulfilment, and a sense of direction to our existence. It involves seeking significance in both the extraordinary and the mundane, and recognising that every moment holds the potential for growth, connection, and personal development.

Here are some insights and strategies to help us discover meaning and purpose in our daily lives:

Embracing Self-Reflection

- **Taking Time for Introspection:** Engaging in self-reflection allows us to connect with our inner selves and gain clarity on our values, passions, and aspirations.

- **Exploring Personal Values:** Identifying the principles and beliefs that are most important to us can guide us in making choices that align with our authentic selves.

- **Examining Life Priorities:** Reflecting on what truly matters to us helps us allocate our time and energy to activities that bring us closer to our purpose.

Finding Meaning in Everyday Activities

- **Mindful Presence:** Cultivating mindfulness allows us to fully engage in the present moment and find beauty and meaning in even the simplest of tasks.

- **Creating a Purposeful Mindset:** Approaching our daily activities with intention and purpose can transform routine tasks into meaningful experiences.

- **Seeking Growth and Learning Opportunities:** Viewing challenges as opportunities for growth and seeking new knowledge and skills enhances our sense of purpose.

Cultivating Connections and Relationships

- **Nurturing Meaningful Relationships:** Building and maintaining positive connections with others fosters a sense of belonging and purpose.

- **Practicing Empathy and Kindness:** By extending compassion and support to others, we contribute to their well-being and create a ripple effect of positivity.

- **Collaborating and Serving a Larger Cause:** Engaging in collective efforts and contributing to a greater purpose can amplify our sense of meaning and impact.

Aligning Work and Passions

- **Discovering Passions and Interests:** Exploring our interests and finding activities that bring us joy and fulfilment helps infuse our daily lives with purpose.

- **Seeking Purpose in Our Careers:** Aligning our work with our values and passions enables us to find meaning in the tasks and contributions we make professionally.

- **Focusing on the Positive Impact:** Shifting our perspective to focus on how our work positively affects others and the world can enhance our sense of purpose.

Embracing Gratitude and Mindfulness

- **Cultivating Gratitude:** Acknowledging and appreciating the blessings and opportunities in our lives fosters a sense of abundance and fulfilment.

- **Practicing Mindfulness:** Being fully present in each moment allows us to notice the richness of our experiences and find meaning in the small details.

- **Engaging in Reflective Practices:** Journaling, meditation, or quiet contemplation can help us deepen our understanding of ourselves and our purpose.

Finding meaning and purpose in everyday life is a continuous and evolving process. It requires us to be open to self-discovery, embrace new perspectives, and remain curious about the world around us. By incorporating these strategies and mindsets into our daily routines, we can infuse our lives with a profound sense of purpose, enrich our relationships, and experience greater fulfilment in our journey. Personal stories of individuals who have found meaning and purpose in their own lives serve as powerful reminders that a purposeful life is within reach for each one of us.

ETERNAL POSITIVITY: INSPIRING PERSONAL STORIES

"Positive relationships are the nourishment of life. Without them, our wellbeing withers."

– Jane Dutton

Ratan Tata: Cultivating the Power of Compassionate Leadership and Innovation

Ratan Tata, one of India's most esteemed industrialists and philanthropists, exemplifies the embodiment of positive energy as a lifelong practice. His personal story is a testament to resilience, determination, and the power of optimism. As the former chairman of the Tata Group, Ratan Tata led the conglomerate with a vision centred on ethical business practices and social responsibility. His commitment to innovation, integrity, and uplifting the lives of people has been the driving force behind his remarkable journey. Tata expressed: *"I don't believe in taking right decisions. I take decisions and then make them right."*

Ratan Tata's unwavering belief in the power of positive energy extends beyond the corporate realm. Through his philanthropic endeavours, such as the Tata Trusts, he has transformed countless lives and contributed to societal development. His initiatives in education, healthcare, and rural development have brought hope and positive change to communities across India. Ratan Tata's compassionate leadership and commitment to making a difference exemplifies the transformative impact of positive energy.

Ratan Tata's personal story and his words of wisdom serve as an inspiration to individuals seeking to make positive energy a lifelong practice. His resilience, humility, and unwavering commitment to creating a positive impact highlight the power of optimism and determination in shaping not only individual success, but also the betterment of society as a whole.

Maya Thompson: Spreading Hope and Kindness

Maya Thompson, a mother who lost her young son to cancer, turned her grief into a mission to spread hope and kindness. Despite the heartbreak, Maya chose to focus on the positive memories and the impact her son had on others' lives. She started a movement called "Ronan's Echo," encouraging random acts of kindness and raising awareness about childhood cancer. Maya's story teaches us that even in the face of tragedy, we can find strength and purpose by channelling our energy into making a positive difference in the world. Maya Thompson says, *"Ronan taught me to love fiercely and to fight for what I believe in. His legacy lives on through acts of kindness, spreading positive energy in his memory."*

David Martinez: Finding Gratitude in Everyday Life

David Martinez, a corporate executive, found himself caught in the cycle of stress and negativity. Feeling overwhelmed, he decided to embark on a journey of self-discovery and began practicing gratitude. Each day, he made a conscious effort to find something to be grateful for, no matter how small. Over time, this simple practice transformed his perspective and allowed him to see the beauty and abundance in his life.

David Martinez reflects, *"Gratitude opened my eyes to the countless blessings surrounding me. It taught me to appreciate the present moment and to find joy in the simplest things. Now, I approach life with a renewed sense of wonder and gratitude."*

Lisa Rodriguez: Embracing the Power of Positive Relationships

Lisa Rodriguez, a social worker, realised the profound impact that positive relationships can have on our overall well-being. After experiencing a challenging period in her life, she decided to prioritise building and nurturing positive connections. She reached out to friends, family, and even joined a support group. Through these relationships, Lisa found a strong support system that uplifted her during difficult times and celebrated her achievements.

Lisa Rodriguez shares, *"Surrounding myself with positive relationships has been transformative. The love, encouragement, and support I receive have fuelled my resilience and helped me maintain a positive outlook on life."*

John Evans: Embracing a Growth Mindset

John Evans, an entrepreneur, faced many setbacks and failures throughout his career. However, instead of allowing them to define him, he embraced a growth mindset. He viewed challenges as opportunities for learning and growth, seeking valuable lessons in each experience. By adopting this perspective, John was able to persevere and ultimately achieve success in his endeavours.

John Evans advises, *"Failure is not the end but a stepping stone towards success. Embrace it, learn from it, and keep moving forward with a positive mindset. Your resilience and determination will propel you to new heights."*

These personal stories serve as powerful reminders that maintaining a positive life is a continuous practice. By finding purpose, cultivating gratitude, fostering positive relationships, and embracing a growth mindset, these individuals have transformed their lives and become beacons of positive energy. Their journeys inspire us to embark on our own paths of self-discovery and growth, reminding us that we have the power to shape our lives through the choices we make and the energy we cultivate.

Incorporate their lessons and experiences into your own life, drawing inspiration from their stories to maintain a sustainable positive life. Remember, you have the capacity to make positivity a lifelong practice and to create a ripple effect of positive energy that can transform not only your own life but also the lives of those around you. As motivational speaker Zig Ziglar once said, *"Positive thinking will let you do everything better than negative thinking will."* Embrace the power of positive energy and let it guide you on a fulfilling and joyful journey.

Amar Bose: Embracing the Power of Passion, Perseverance and Innovation

Amar Bose was an influential Indian-American engineer and entrepreneur who founded the audio equipment company Bose Corporation. He is known for his pioneering work in audio technology and his commitment to delivering high-quality sound experiences.

Amar Bose's story is a testament to the transformative power of passion, perseverance, and innovation. He was driven by a deep curiosity and a desire to improve the way people experience music and sound. Through his relentless pursuit of excellence, he revolutionised the audio industry with groundbreaking inventions and advancements.

Through his innovative contributions to the field of audio technology, he brought joy and inspiration to people worldwide. Bose believed in the transformative power of positive energy and how it could enhance communication and learning among individuals. He expressed: *"I'm a great believer that any tool that enhances communication has profound effects in terms of how people can learn from each other, and how they can achieve the kind of freedoms that they're interested in."*

His relentless pursuit of excellence and dedication to creating immersive and transformative music experiences reflected his commitment to spreading positive energy.

Narendra Modi: Positivity through Empowerment & Transformative Leadership

Narendra Modi, the Prime Minister of India, is known for his charismatic leadership and his ability to inspire millions through his positive energy. He has demonstrated the practice of positive energy as a way of life, both in his personal journey and in his governance. Modi's belief in The Power of Optimism & Self-Love has been instrumental in overcoming challenges and driving positive change. His vision of a prosperous and inclusive India is fuelled by his unwavering positive energy and his commitment to empowering individuals and communities. He quotes: "*I'm a very optimistic person. I always believe that the best is yet to come.*"

Narendra Modi's emphasis on positive energy extends beyond his personal journey. As a leader, he has focused on fostering a culture of positivity and empowerment, encouraging individuals to tap into their inherent potential. Through his initiatives such as "Make in India," "Swachh Bharat Abhiyan" (Clean India Campaign), and "Digital India," Modi has demonstrated his unwavering commitment to transforming India into a progressive and inclusive nation. His positive energy resonates with people from all walks of life, inspiring them to embrace positivity and work towards a brighter future. Modi reflects: *"Hard work never brings fatigue. It brings satisfaction."*

Narendra Modi's personal story and his words of wisdom serve as an inspiration to individuals who strive to make positive energy a lifelong practice. His relentless optimism, dedication to service, and transformative leadership highlight the power of positive energy in shaping not only individual lives, but also the destiny of a nation.

11
CULTIVATING POSITIVITY WITH EVERYDAY THINGS

"Life is really amazing when you can amaze yourself with simple things"

– Debasish Mridha

In our journey towards cultivating a positive life, we often overlook the potential of everyday mundane things that surround us. However, it is important to recognise that even the simplest aspects of our lives can contribute to the overall culture of positivity. By shifting our perspective and infusing positivity into the ordinary, we can transform our experiences and create a more uplifting environment.

As we have seen in this book, one powerful way to harness the potential of everyday, mundane things is through gratitude and mindfulness. Taking a moment to appreciate the little things, such as the warmth of sunlight streaming through a window or the aroma of a freshly brewed cup of coffee, can help us cultivate a sense of gratitude and presence in the present moment. By consciously savouring these small joys, we infuse positivity into our daily lives and enhance our overall well-being.

Another way to cultivate positivity through mundane things is by incorporating intentional rituals into our daily routines. These rituals can be as simple as starting the day with a positive affirmation, taking a few moments to stretch and breathe deeply, or creating a calming evening routine before bed. By infusing our routines with mindful and positive actions, we set a tone of positivity for the day and create moments of self-care and reflection.

USING ARTS, COLOURS, SPACE DESIGN, AND CLOTHING

"Colours, like features, follow the changes of emotions."

— Pablo Picasso

Art has the incredible ability to touch our souls, evoke emotions, and inspire us in profound ways. Scientific research conducted by positive psychologists has shown that exposure to art can elicit positive emotions, enhance well-being, and even reduce stress levels (Hass-Cohen & Carr, 2008). Whether it's a captivating painting, a moving piece of music, or a thought-provoking sculpture, art has the unique ability to transcend words and connect with our innermost selves.

As we surround ourselves with art that resonates with us, we invite its positive energy into our lives. Choose artwork that speaks to your heart, ignites your imagination, and aligns with your values. It could be a vibrant abstract painting that fills your space with energy and joy, a serene landscape that brings a sense of tranquillity, or a piece of inspirational typography that reminds you of your strength and resilience. Let art be a reflection of your authentic self and a source of inspiration that uplifts your spirit and spreads positive vibes for all who encounter it.

Colours also play a significant role in shaping our emotions and energy. Countless studies have explored the psychological impact of colours on our mood and well-being. For example, research has shown that warm colours like yellow and orange can evoke feelings of happiness, optimism, and creativity, while cool colours like blue and green can promote a sense of calm, relaxation, and balance (Elliot & Maier, 2014; Kwallek et al., 1997). By intentionally incorporating colours that resonate with us into our living spaces, we can create an environment that nurtures positive energy.

Consider the colours you surround yourself with and how they make you feel. Infuse your space with hues that uplift your mood and align with the atmosphere you wish to cultivate. Perhaps you choose a sunny yellow for your kitchen to stimulate feelings of warmth and joy during meal preparation, or a calming blue for your bedroom to promote restful sleep and relaxation. Let colours be a vibrant expression of your personality and an invitation for positive energy to flow freely in your surroundings.

Space design goes hand in hand with colours and plays a crucial role in creating an environment that fosters positivity. Our physical spaces have the power to influence our emotions, mindset, and overall well-being. When we enter a cluttered and disorganised space, we may feel overwhelmed and stressed, hindering our ability to experience positive emotions. On the other hand, a well-designed and harmonious space can promote a sense of peace, clarity, and focus.

Take a moment to assess your living and working spaces. Are there areas that could benefit from decluttering and organising? Create a serene and balanced environment by finding a place for everything and ensuring that objects align with your values and bring you joy. Introduce elements of nature, such as plants or natural materials, to connect with the calming energy of the outdoors. Enhance natural light and ventilation to create a fresh and invigorating atmosphere. Let your space be a sanctuary that nurtures your well-being and radiates positive energy from everyone who enters.

Our clothing choices also contribute to the positive energy we exude. What we wear can significantly impact our self-perception, confidence, and interactions with others. When we dress in clothes that make us feel comfortable, confident, and authentic, we radiate a positive aura that attracts positivity from others. Choose clothing that reflects your personal style and makes you feel empowered. Whether it's a vibrant outfit that energises your day, a well-tailored suit that boosts your confidence in professional settings, or casual attire that allows you to relax and be yourself, let your clothing be an expression of your true self. When we feel good in our own skin, our positive energy shines through, uplifting not only ourselves but also those we encounter. As fashion designer Rachel Zoe aptly stated, *"Style is a way to say who you are without having to speak."* Let us embrace clothing that makes us feel comfortable, confident, and aligned with our true selves.

LITTLE TWEAKS CAN CHANGE A LOT OF THINGS

Incorporating arts, colours, and space design into our lives with intentionality allows us to create an environment that cultivates and spreads positive energy. By surrounding ourselves with art that inspires us, colours that uplift our spirits, spaces that promote peace and harmony, and clothing that reflect our authenticity, we invite positivity to flow into every aspect of our lives. Let your environment and personal expression become powerful tools in your journey towards a more positive and fulfilling existence.

I encourage you to reflect on the following quote by Pablo Picasso: *"Colours, like features, follow the changes of emotions."* Let the colours, art, design, and clothing you choose to be a reflection of the positive emotions and energy you wish to embody. Embrace the power of your surroundings and personal expression to create a life filled with positivity, inspiration, and joy.

SPREADING POSITIVE ENERGY: THE POWER OF SIMPLE ACTIONS

Our actions, no matter how small, have the power to create a positive ripple effect in the world. By consciously choosing kindness, compassion, and positivity in our interactions with others, we can spread positive energy and inspire others to do the same. Simple acts of kindness, such as offering a helping hand, giving compliments, actively listening to others, and standing up for the right things, can make a significant impact on someone's day and contribute to a more positive and supportive community.

Our attitude and mindset can also influence the energy we bring to our interactions. By approaching situations with an open mind, a willingness to learn and grow, and a positive outlook, we create an environment that encourages collaboration, understanding, and empathy. Our words and actions have the power to uplift, inspire, and motivate those around us, and by consciously choosing positivity, we can be catalysts for positive change.

In brevity, recognising the potential of everyday things, incorporating positivity into our environment through art, colours, space design, and clothing, and spreading positive energy through our simple actions, we can create a culture of positivity that permeates our lives and the world around us. Each small step we take contributes to a greater collective shift towards a more uplifting and harmonious existence. Let us embrace the power within us to turn things around and make a positive difference in our lives and the lives of others.

HARNESSING THE POWER OF MUSIC FOR POSITIVE VIBES

Music has a profound impact on our emotions and can be a powerful tool for creating a positive atmosphere. Here are two subtopics that delve deeper into the significance of music:

The Healing Power of Music

Music has been used for centuries as a form of therapy and healing. It has the ability to uplift our spirits, soothe our minds, and evoke powerful emotions. When we listen to uplifting and positive music, it can have a transformative effect on our well-being. The rhythm, melody, and lyrics can inspire us, bring solace during challenging times, and energise us with positivity. Whether it's through playing an instrument, singing, or simply enjoying our favourite tunes, music can serve as a gateway to a more positive and harmonious state of being.

Spreading Positivity through Musical Acts

Music has a unique ability to bring people together and create a sense of unity and joy. We can harness this power to spread positive energy to the world around us through musical acts. This can involve organising community singing or jam sessions, participating in local music events, or even performing random acts of music in public spaces. By sharing our musical talents and engaging others in the joy of music, we can create moments of connection, uplift spirits, and inspire positivity in others. Music has the power to transcend boundaries, language barriers, and cultural differences, making it a universal language of positivity and harmony.

By exploring the impact of music and incorporating it into our lives, we can enhance our own well-being and contribute to a more positive and harmonious world. Let the rhythm, melodies, and harmonies of music infuse your daily life with positive energy and inspire those around you to embrace the power of music for a more vibrant and uplifting existence.

CONCLUSION

"The only way to grow is by embracing challenges, persisting in the face of setbacks, and seeing effort as the path to mastery."

– Carol Dweck

I n conclusion, throughout this book, we have explored the transformative power of positive energy and its profound impact on our lives. We have delved into various aspects of cultivating positivity, including mindset, self-love, gratitude, resilience, connection, purpose, and maintaining a sustainable positive life. These key points, when applied consistently and intentionally, can bring about remarkable changes in our lives.

To apply these principles to your own life, remember the following:

- **Mindset Matters:** Cultivate a positive mindset by challenging negative thoughts, embracing self-belief, and reframing challenges as opportunities for growth.

- **Self-Love and Gratitude:** Practice self-love by nurturing a deep appreciation for yourself and cultivating gratitude for the blessings in your life. Embrace the power of gratitude to shift your perspective and invite abundance.

- **Resilience and Adaptability:** Develop resilience by embracing failures as stepping stones to success and maintaining a growth mindset. Adapt to change and view challenges as opportunities for personal growth and learning.

- **Connection and Community:** Foster positive relationships and seek a connection with others. Surround yourself with individuals who uplift and support you on your journey. Embrace the power of community and contribute to the well-being of others.

- **Purpose and Meaning:** Discover your purpose and align your actions with your values. Live a purpose-driven life that brings fulfilment and joy, knowing that your contributions matter.

✧ **Sustainable Positive Life:** Implement practical tips and techniques to maintain a sustainable positive life. Set aside time for self-reflection, be open to new experiences, and persevere in the face of challenges.

As you embark on your own journey of positivity, remember that transformation takes time and consistency. Embrace these principles as daily practices and watch as they shape your life in extraordinary ways. I also encourage you to share your own stories of transformation and growth. By sharing your experiences, you inspire others and create a ripple effect of positivity. Your story has the power to touch lives and ignite change in those who read or hear it.

In closing, I invite you to embrace positivity and self-love as a daily practice. Embrace the power within you to create a life filled with joy, purpose, and meaningful connections. You have the ability to shape your reality and become a beacon of positive energy. Embrace this journey, celebrate your progress, and let your light shine brightly. Remember, the world needs your unique brand of positivity.

In conclusion, I would like to extend my heartfelt gratitude to each and every reader who has joined me on this remarkable journey through the pages of this book. Your time and attention are invaluable, and I sincerely hope that the ideas, stories, and insights shared within these chapters have resonated with you.

If you found this book to be thought-provoking, inspiring, or informative, I kindly ask for your support. Your feedback and reviews are essential in spreading the message and impact of this work to a wider audience. By sharing your thoughts and impressions, you not only contribute to the growth of the book, but also provide valuable guidance to potential readers.

Your honest reviews on platforms such as Goodreads, Amazon, or any other platform of your choice can make a tremendous difference. Let others know how this book has influenced your thinking, touched your heart, or inspired positive change in your life. Your review will not only help me, but will also help other readers discover the book and embark on their own transformative journey.

Once again, thank you for being a part of this incredible adventure. I am deeply grateful for your support, and I look forward to hearing your thoughts and seeing the impact this book has had on your life. Together, let us continue to spread the power of knowledge, inspiration, and growth.

REFERENCES

Brown, B. (2010). The Gifts of Imperfection: Let Go of Who You Think You're Supposed to Be and Embrace Who You Are. Hazelden Publishing.

Csikszentmihalyi, M. (1990). Flow: The psychology of optimal experience. Harper & Row.

Dutton, J. E. (2003). Energise your workplace: How to build and sustain high-quality connections at work. Jossey-Bass.

Dweck, C. S. (2006). Mindset: The new psychology of success. Random House.

Dutton, J. E. (2019). The Oxford Handbook of Positive Organisational Scholarship. Oxford University Press.

Emmons, R. A., & McCullough, M. E. (2003). Counting blessings versus burdens: An experimental investigation of gratitude and subjective well-being in daily life. Journal of Personality and Social Psychology, 84(2), 377-389.

Frankl, V. E. (2006). Man's Search for Meaning. Beacon Press.

Fredrickson, B. L. (2001). The role of positive emotions in positive psychology: The broaden-and-build theory of positive emotions. American psychologist, 56(3), 218-226.

Froh, J. J., Sefick, W. J., & Emmons, R. A. (2008). Counting blessings in early adolescents: An experimental study of gratitude and subjective well-being. Journal of School Psychology, 46(2), 213-233.

Groeschel, C. (2018). Divine Direction: 7 Decisions That Will Change Your Life. Zondervan.

Jain, S., Hebert, J. R., & Mills, P. J. (2015). Heart rate variability and psychosocial factors in patients with hypertension. Integrative Medicine Research, 4(4), 196-202.

Jakes, T. D. (2017). Destiny: Step into Your Purpose. FaithWords.

Jimenez, T. R., Hoffman, A., & Grant, J. (2011). Exploring the relationship between purpose in life, social connectedness, and positive and negative affect in a diverse sample. Journal of Positive Psychology, 6(3), 197-208.

Kabat-Zinn, J. (1990). Full catastrophe living: Using the wisdom of your body and mind to face stress, pain, and illness. Random House.

Keltner, D. (2009). Born to be good: The science of a meaningful life. WW Norton & Company.

Keltner, D. (2019). The power paradox: How we gain and lose influence. Penguin.

Lyubomirsky, S., Sheldon, K. M., & Schkade, D. (2005). Pursuing Happiness: The Architecture of Sustainable Change. Review of General Psychology, 9(2), 111-131.

Lyubomirsky, S., Sousa, L., & Dickerhoof, R. (2006). The costs and benefits of writing, talking, and thinking about life's triumphs and defeats. Journal of Personality and Social Psychology, 90(4), 692-708.

Maraboli, S. (2013). Unapologetically You: Reflections on Life and the Human Experience. Amazon Digital Services LLC.

Ortberg, J. (2014). Soul keeping: Caring for the most important part of you. Zondervan.

Ortberg, J. (2017). The Me I Want to Be: Becoming God's Best Version of You. Zondervan.

Seligman, M. E., Steen, T. A., Park, N., & Peterson, C. (2005). Positive psychology progress: Empirical validation of interventions. American Psychologist, 60(5), 410-421.

Seligman, M. E. (2011). Flourish: A visionary new understanding of happiness and well-being. Simon and Schuster.

Sheldon, K. M., & Lyubomirsky, S. (2006). How to increase and sustain positive emotion: The effects of expressing gratitude and visualising best possible selves. Journal of Positive Psychology, 1(2), 73–82. doi: 10.1080/17439760500510676.

Tang, Y. Y., Hölzel, B. K., & Posner, M. I. (2015). The neuroscience of mindfulness meditation. Nature Reviews Neuroscience, 16(4), 213-225.

Warren, R. (2002). The purpose-driven life: What on earth am I here for? Zondervan.

Wood, A. M., Froh, J. J., & Geraghty, A. W. (2010). Gratitude and well-being: A review and theoretical integration. Clinical Psychology Review, 30(7), 890-905.

ACKNOWLEDGEMENTS

I am filled with immense gratitude as I reflect on the journey of creating this book, "Positive Energy Positive Life: The Power of Optimism & Self-Love." It is with heartfelt appreciation that I acknowledge the individuals who have played an integral role in bringing this project to fruition.

First and foremost, I would like to express my deep gratitude to my family and loved ones for their unwavering support and understanding throughout this endeavour. Their encouragement, belief in my abilities, and unconditional love have been my anchor during the challenging moments, and I am forever grateful.

I am indebted to my editor, Paul Earnest, whose keen eye, expertise, and valuable feedback have enhanced the clarity and cohesiveness of the content. His dedication to excellence and commitment to bringing out the best in this book is truly commendable.

I extend my heartfelt gratitude to my dear friend, Mike Aldridge, for his unwavering support and infectious positivity throughout this book's creation. Your belief in me and this project has consistently inspired, providing the energy to overcome challenges and doubts. Your friendship and positive energy have profoundly impacted my life, and I am honoured to have you by my side on this remarkable journey. Thank you, Mike, for being a radiant light and sharing your uplifting spirit with me.

In the tapestry of this literary journey, I owe an immeasurable debt of gratitude to my valued friend Leigh Morphies. Her unwavering support has been my rock, her encouragement my guiding light. With boundless enthusiasm and a wealth of invaluable insights, she propelled me forward on this creative odyssey. To Leigh, whose ideas breathed life into these pages, I offer my deepest thanks, for her influence is woven into the very fabric of this book, making it all the more vibrant and profound.

To Olga, a cherished soul who resides close to the core of my heart, I extend my profound gratitude. Her unwavering support and belief in my abilities have been the bedrock upon which this book stands. Throughout the journey, she has been an unceasing source of motivation, reminding me of my potential when doubt threatened to overshadow it. Thank you, Olga, for being the driving force behind the completion of this book.

In the constellation of gratitude, I shine a special light on Shafi Choudhury, a cherished family friend and enduring source of inspiration for over a decade. His indirect influence on my life has been immeasurable, and our past collaboration, which I hold as an honour, was more than a professional alliance—it was a lifeline during challenging times. I am forever indebted to him for his invaluable mentorship, a beacon that guided my journey. Shafi Choudhury, your lasting impact is woven into the fabric of this book, and for that, my gratitude knows no bounds.

Special thanks are owed to my childhood friend Bhavneet Thukral, whose steadfast support and friendship have ignited my creative spirit and instilled unshakable confidence. Your presence in my life has brought boundless inspiration and positivity, empowering me to push beyond my limits. Bhavneet, I am deeply grateful for your invaluable friendship and the impact you've had on my journey of self-discovery and creativity. Thank you for being a constant source of inspiration and support.

To my dear friend, Parminderjit Samra. Your friendship and support have been instrumental in my personal and professional growth. Your belief in my abilities and constant encouragement have infused me with a newfound confidence and resolute determination. Thank you Parminderjit, I am grateful for your wisdom and support.

To the researchers, psychologists, and experts whose groundbreaking work forms the foundation of this book, I express my sincere gratitude. Their invaluable insights, research findings, and expertise have helped shape the concepts and ideas within these pages, making this a comprehensive and informative resource.

To the readers of this book, I extend my heartfelt appreciation. Your interest in personal growth and your commitment to cultivating positive energy and self-love inspire me. It is my sincere hope that the words within these pages resonate with you, providing guidance, motivation, and support on your own journey to living a more positive and fulfilling life.

In conclusion, I am humbled and honoured to have had the opportunity to write this book. It would not have been possible without the collective efforts, love, and support of those mentioned above, as well as many others who have touched my life along the way.